BALLAD COUNTRY

The Scottish Border

BALLAD COUNTRY

The Scottish Border

MADGE ELDER

F.S.A. (Scot.)

OLIVER & BOYD

EDINBURGH AND LONDON

OLIVER AND BOYD LTD
Tweeddale Court
Edinburgh 1

39a Welbeck Street
London W.1

First published 1963

© 1963 Madge Elder
Printed in Great Britain
by Robert MacLehose & Co. Ltd, Glasgow

For

MARGERY VIRTUE TURNBULL

with love and gratitude

Preface

I HAVE CALLED this book *Ballad Country*, but I do not, of course,
claim the Border Line region of which I write as exclusively the
Ballad Country. But it has always been particularly associated
with the traditional ballads, and it remains so today. There is
scarcely a Border poet who has not felt the influence of the ballad
and attempted some of his own.

I have taken the old Scottish Border ballads and related them to
their historical and geographical background, sketched in a brief
history of the clans and families involved, and attempted to depict
the metamorphosis of the moss-trooper.

The ballads of Ettrick, Yarrow and the Merse have been
omitted because I have already covered that region in a previous
book. Although my wanderings took me over the Border line to the
English side and down to the Roman Wall, I realised it would be
impossible within the scope of this book to cover equally the English
Border ballads. They would require a volume to themselves.

There is today a greater interest in the ballad than ever before.
It is being realised that they are a branch of social study. They
were not poems; but words set to an air; and the originals were
sometimes coarser and have been refined down the years by
successive editors. I have therefore relied chiefly on versions in
Child's marvellous collection.

But it has not been my aim to write a thesis on the ballad. Mine
was a light-hearted journey undertaken for the sheer joy of it, and
in the hope that others would make their own explorations in this
Border ballad country and find my book not a guide book but a
companionable guide.

I should have liked to thank all who helped me on my journey,
whether by supplying me with information, or in any other way;
and although, alas! there are many of them whose names I never
learnt, I most gratefully recall their friendliness.

For permission to visit the historic houses of Branxholme,
Harden, Harwood, and Thirlestane, I am especially indebted to
the Duke of Buccleuch, to Lord Polwarth, to Baroness Elliot, and to
Commander Napier. I am also very grateful: to Baroness Elliot,

to the Hon. Mrs Napier, and to the Hon. Mrs Scott of High-chesters, who themselves showed me round; to Capt. and Mrs Milne Home, for granting me the privilege of wandering beside that beautiful stretch of Esk in the grounds of Irvine House; to the Duke and Duchess of Roxburghe, for lending me two valuable books from Floors Castle; to Commander Napier, to Mrs Palmer Douglas, and to Miss Dorothy Turnbull, for letting me see private family histories; to Miss Sylvia Steuart, for letting me see the Bell family history; to Mrs Cowan, for letting me see that of the Logan-Home family history; to Baroness Elliot, for showing me her notes on the Harwood charters; to Mr Alexander Irvine, for showing me his notes on the Irvine family, and on the Turnbulls in France; to Mr Horace and Miss Hetha St Paul Butler, Miss Augusta Leishman, Major Askew, for the use of many other family and local books; to Mr John Byers, for the use of his own book, *Liddesdale*; and to Miss Hetha St Paul Butler, for introducing me to the lovely Glen at Ewart Park.

With the deepest gratitude I also recall the immense amount of help and encouragement that I received from Sir John McEwen and Sir Gordon Lethem, two kindly Scots who both died before this work reached the proof-stage. For all useful information that they ungrudgingly gave me, I wish also to thank: Lady Lethem; Lady Bridget McEwen; Mrs Malcolm, Eskdalemuir; Mrs Graham, Langholm; Miss Falla, Southdean Schoolhouse; Mr W. Robson-Scott, Reader at London University; Mr Brown, Yetholm Schoolhouse; Mr Renwick, Upper Chatto; Mr Cunningham, Coldstream; Mr Wyllie, Branxholme; Mr Tom Graham, Rothesay; Miss M. Armstrong, Mrs Waugh, and Mrs Wood, Canonbie; and the Parish Ministers of Yetholm, Linton, and Ladykirk. I am particularly grateful to the Town Clerk of Langholm, for much useful information and advice, and to the Town Crier, for delineating the exact boundaries of the Debatable Land.

But for the kindness of friends with cars, I could not have covered nearly so much ground in the time I had set myself; and for the transport that they so kindly provided I owe a special debt of gratitude: to the Misses Jean and Isabel Speedy; to Mrs Bluitt (daughter of the late Mr Brand the Woller antiquarian) and her sisters, who all also provided much information; to my cousin Ella Grierson; to Mr Robert Mathison; and to Miss G. Todd.

My old schoolmate Mrs Hislop, Raperlaw, the first English
Borderer I ever knew, acted as guide to her native Norham; and
to her I owe much.

My " Teri " guide, Jean Virtue deserves a special word of ap-
preciation for the indefatigable labours by which she tracked down
the " old pedlar's family tree "; and so does Mrs Miller, Hawick,
for kindly allowing me to borrow it.   This interesting document
purports to trace the descendants of Siward of the Strong Arm
down through the Lairds of Mangerton to Johnie of Gilnockie,
Christie's Will of the Hollows, and other redoubtable Armstrongs,
but ends, in London and Ireland, in 1684.   To Miss Jean Cunningham, Edinburgh, to Mrs Paul Mefford Runyon, Washington,
D.C., and to Miss Virginia Jeffrey Smith, Rochester, N.Y., who
all claim to be collaterally descended from Johnie of Gilnockie, I
am very grateful for much interesting information that they have
given me, and for all the enquiries that they have made in the hope
of furnishing me with clues to any living descendants.   They,
perhaps, are not the only claimants, yet I am bound to say that I
have not found any who can prove direct descent.

The Librarians of Kelso, Hawick, and Galashiels were " ready,
aye ready," to help me in my researches.   In the Reference Room
of the Library of Galashiels, I spent many fascinating hours with
the *Calendar of Border Papers*; and whenever I lifted my eyes and
looked out of the window, the sight of Lorimer's Pele Tower and
Clapperton's Mosstrooper spurred me on to further effort.   And
with much gratitude I also recall the encouragement and inspira-
tion that Major the Hon. Henry Douglas Home gave me when, in
Yarrow, he and I took part with Dr Francis Collinson in a B.B.C.
broadcast called " Ballads of the Border Watch Towers."

I am grateful to the Editors of *The Scotsman*, *The Weekly Scotsman*,
Scotland's Magazine, *Scots Magazine*, and *Southern Annual* for permis-
sion to reprint material which first appeared in those periodicals.
Acknowledgments are due to the following for permission to repro-
duce quotations from the works indicated: Longmans, Green &
Co. Ltd (Trevalyan: *A History of England*, and *A Layman's Love of
Letters*);   The World's Work (1913) Ltd (John Mackay: *Knowing
Scotland*); Dr C. M. Grieve and Oliver and Boyd Ltd (*The Collected
Poems of Hugh MacDiarmid*); Oliver and Boyd Ltd (R. L. Mackie:
King James IV of Scotland);   Miss Rhoda Spence (Lewis Spence:
" The Scots Glamourie," in *The Scots Companion*, of which she was

editor). And for permission to quote some other copyright material I have to thank Will H. Ogilvie and Carver Collins.

Also, I wish to thank the publishers' editorial staff for their care and consideration and helpfulness at all times. Neither would I omit my typist Miss Shanks for her heroic tackling of the wording of the old ballads!

M.E.

Contents

Photographs

Maps

PRELUDE

The Border Line

ONE OF THE MOST exciting frontiers in the world is that hundred and ten miles which separates the two kingdoms of Scotland and England, and is known as the Border line. It was almost a visible line to me. Our farm, which lay on the edge of the Lammermuirs, looked out over the Merse, the old East March, to the great barrier of the Cheviots along which much of its course lay. I knew it also as ballad country, for we were brought up on the ballads. Our mother used to sing them to us. She had a lovely voice and a wonderful sense of the drama inherent in the old ballads. Long before I ever explored a mile of that country it was very real to me, as familiar in the mind as the plains of " windy Troy." Our great-uncle was an old Scots dominie and a great Greek scholar and from him my elder sister used to hear the stories of the Greek myths and heroes of the Homeric lays, which she regaled to me, and the two sets of legends and heroes became inextricably mixed up in my young mind.

In his book *The Border Line*, published in 1924, Logan Mack described how he had explored it on foot from end to end—much of it up in the highest Cheviots—and it had taken him, in stages, more than six years. I had spent all of ten years covering my own line of country, when searching out the line of Pele Towers " from Berwick to the Bield,"—another historic hundred miles. Often I had looked out from some eminence on that distant Border line " whose margin fades for ever and for ever when I move " and wondered if I should ever compass it.

I am no great hill-climber, nor could I afford another decade to follow the actual line, which would take me up at times into the 2,000 foot range. There remained the lower level, the " green roads " through the foothills, the lonely tracks over moss and moor, even the metalled roads that now run so closely to the Border that they cross it at several points. I would be following in the very trail of the ballads.

Five years drifted past. But in the end, inevitably, I made the journey.

I

" The Muckle Toon "

I CAME TO Langholm in a " Liddesdale drowe," a moist mist too
fine to be called rain or even a drizzle.

The first person I met was an Armstrong, who was also the
Town Clerk. This was arresting. I was on the trail of " Johnie
Armstrong." But he laid no claim to direct descent from that
notorious freebooter.

When I mentioned I wanted to see the Common Riding he gave
me a programme. The number of old Eskdale names still represented among the committee and officials—Elliots, Beatties,
Irvings, Littles, Bells, Maxwells, Johnstones, MacVitties, etc.—
was impressive.

Mr Armstrong warned me that it would be extremely difficult,
perhaps impossible, to get accommodation for the following week
of the Common Riding, as every place was usually booked up, often
months beforehand. It is a great " clan gathering," a purely
family affair, and a principal home-coming for exiles. The
stranger, the tourist, must take his chance. I asked for a list of
" Accommodation." Mr Armstrong said there was none.

" Some time ago," he said, " we advertised and did not get one
reply."

This is typical of the Borderer. He is not really interested in
commercialising the great romantic and historical assets, and the
undoubted beauty, of his country. You might think he was not
himself greatly interested in such. He seems completely absorbed
in his farms—and his tweed and woollen mills. But wait. Watch
him at one of his Common Ridings, or great traditional festivals,
and you will discover that the old fire is not dead, that the old
ballads are still sung.

The Town Clerk was right. I found that every place was
booked up. But what started as a hunt for accommodation turned
into an absorbing exploration of an old Border burgh town, whose

[3]

history lies at the very roots of the Common Riding celebrations and is important to an understanding of it.

I started at the " Townhead." This is the oldest part of Langholm, known in the fourteenth and fifteenth centuries as " Arkinholm." Here at Eweswaterfoot was one of the principal fords which linked the Kilngreen and the Castleholm (or Muckle Kilngreen) common lands. It was on the Kilngreen the old fairs were held, and the modern shows are now pitched.

These fairs existed, of course, in Saxon times but became more important under the Normans. The right to grant a fair was one of the royal prerogatives. It was granted mostly to religious houses and the great feudal lords. The fair would be " cried " at the Mercat Cross in front of the Tollbooth before the tolls could be collected; " tolls " for articles sold; " stallage " for the liberty to erect stalls; " package " payment to the owner of the ground on which the stall was erected and dismantled. An official was appointed to keep order, and a pillory provided for offenders.

Langholm's growth from free barony to burgh began in 1610 with the granting of a charter by the king to Lord William Cranston; in 1621 by another charter to Lord Nithsdale with right to hold fairs, and on his forfeiture, the lands passed to the Buccleuchs.

The history of the burghers, in Langholm, as elsewhere was a perpetual struggle to preserve their rights to the common lands, and it was to protect these that boundary lines were defined by natural features, or ditches and cairns. A man was employed to examine the boundary line each year, and from 1765 the town crier, Archibald Beattie, perambulated the burgh marches for fifty years, usually on the day following the excitement of the big annual fair in July.

Border history is largely the rise of one noble house on the fall of another, and of the greatest to hold sway in Eskdale were the Douglases, 1319–1455; the Maxwells, 1455–1643; the Buccleuchs, from 1643.

The Battle of Arkinholm marked the fall of the great House of Douglas which had dominated the Borders since the Bruce had given lands to his faithful adherent and friend the " good lord James." The Maxwells rose in their place, to become famous Wardens of the March. On the Castleholm are the fragmentary remains of their castle, which they often granted to an Armstrong in league with them. Or rather it might be said the Maxwells

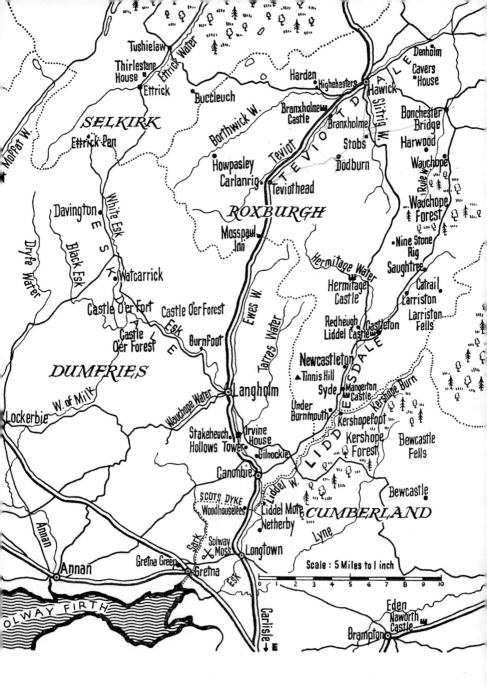

Roxburghshire, Dumfriesshire, Selkirkshire, and
County of Cumberland.

B

turned a blind eye to the Armstrong raids. The Armstrongs in their turn were not above " hunting " with the Scottish Warden and " riding " with his English opposite number, and certainly were a plague to both.

It was at the Castleholm, the ballad of " Johnie Armstrong " tells:

> The Elliots and the Armstrangs did convene,
>> They were a gallant companie. . . .
>
> They ran their horse on the Langum *ᵃ*howm,   *ᵃ flat ground beside a river*
>> And brake their speirs with *ᵇ*mekle main; *ᵇ much*
> The ladies lukit frae their loft-windows:
>> " God bring our men *ᶜ*weil back again! "   *ᶜ well*

Tradition says that only one survivor returned to tell the fate of Johnie Armstrong and his men, and to warn the occupiers of the Castle. They fled to the wilds of Tarras Moss.

But I would have to go to Gilnockie, and the graveyard of Carlanrig, to trace the beginning and end of that story.

Maxwell, Lord Nithsdale, forfeited his estates for his adherence to the royalist cause and his lands were given to Buccleuch. The " Bold Buccleuch " brought romance; and Anne, Duchess of Buccleuch and Monmouth, and the third Duke—" farmer Duke " —brought progress and prosperity to their tenants. That beneficent influence has continued to this day.

Langholm is not a large place compared with such mill towns as Hawick and Galashiels, and the name " Muckle Toon o' Langholm " puzzles many. But at one time it was actually larger than these two towns combined.

In no other Border town, although nearly all are beside a river, had I seen so many bridges. Appropriate, one might think, to the town where the great bridge-builder, Telford, served his apprenticeship to a local builder.

Crossing one of these bridges I found myself in Stubholm—the birthplace of another celebrated Armstrong. Archie Armstrong, like all his clan, was a noted freebooter, but he turned the dry wit of the Borderer to such good account that he was appointed Court Jester to James VI and later to Charles I. Archie's long feud with Archbishop Laud is a matter of history.

I had walked from Townhead to Townfoot, up the Kirk Wynd

and along the drove road—the route the Common Riding procession would take—before I returned to the square to wait for my
bus back to Melrose. The stage was set, but it seemed I was not to
see the drama played out. The decorations were already going up.
I could sense the air of mounting excitement. It was here in the
square that the ceremonies would commence—here where the old
fairs were " cried " at the Mercat Cross.

I had enjoyed my day in Langholm, in spite of the " Liddesdale
drowe " and my fruitless search. Everyone had been friendly and
as helpful as possible—I had been kindly directed from one place
to another. Langholm itself seemed a very pleasant town in a
beautiful setting.

> Arrived at Langholm at about five o'clock [wrote Dorothy Words-
> worth in her *Journal of a Tour in Scotland*]. The town, as we ap-
> proached it, from a hill, looked very pretty, the houses being roofed
> with blue slates, standing close to the Esk, here a large river, that
> scattered its waters wide over a stoney channel. The Inn neat and
> comfortable, exceedingly clean. I could hardly believe we were
> still in Scotland.

The sting was in the tail. And with that Dorothy crossed the
Border line to her own side.

I had made up my mind to return for the actual Common Riding Day, which is the culmination of a week's celebrations, even if
it meant being, like the reivers, " out before the dawn and home
behind the stars." But during the week came a telephone call
offering me a bed at Hartmanor, a farm about half-way up
Eskdalemuir. That was at least nearer than Melrose; though I
would have to leave the house by car about 5.15 a.m. to be in time
for the hound trails.

The mists were low on the hills and there was a smirr of rain as
we raced through the valley. The cattle and sheep were still lying
down in the fields and lifted sleepy eyes, but Langholm town was
already wide awake when we arrived, and the people were astir in
the streets. They had been awakened by the Flute Band at 5 a.m.
All the Border Common Ridings begin early. This may be a relic
of the days when the people had few holidays. Here the " hinds "
(farm servants) were hired on the understanding that they got two
days off, one for the Canonbie Sacrament and the other for the
Common Riding.

There was a steady stream of cars going up the road on the flank of Whita Hill, and the temporary car park about half-way up was already filled. There was an estimated crowd of 2,000 on the hill at the starting-point. The hounds were arriving by car and brake and being assembled in a field a little below the road, thirty-two of them. They are a breed of foxhounds but never allowed to hunt. They were straining at their leashes and bringing down more than one of their masters in the rough ground, but one elderly man approached the starting line with slow deliberation, his hound strictly to heel. He was the last to reach the line, not a moment too soon. I would have been prepared to say that dog would be the winner—if I could have told one from the other when the race began.

Then they were off—white lightning streaks against the dark moss. In a few moments they were out of sight in a hollow. Their owners began to leave the field. A catering van was doing a tremendous trade in the traditional pies.

The dogs would not be seen again for about half an hour. I had time to look about and think. . . . This was harmless sport now, but in old times it was a grimmer business in these hills—outlaws " put to the horn " (three blasts of a horn declared an outlaw) and tracked down by bloodhounds—by " hound and horn " as the phrase went, and as described in " Hobie Noble," a ballad of this very region:

> Now Hobie he was an English man,
> And born into Bewcastle dale,
> But his misdeeds were they sae great,
> They banished him to Liddisdale.

> At Kershope-foot the *a*tryst was set,   *a rendezvous*
> Kershope of the *b*lily lee;   *b lovely lea*
> And there was traitor Sim o the Mains,
> With him a private companie.

> The Hobie has *a*graithed his body weel,   *a equipped*
> I wat it was wi' baith good iron and steel;
> And he has pull'd out his fringed grey,
> And there, brave Noble, he rade him weel. . . .

> Then word is gane to the land-sergeant,
> In Askirton where that he lay;

" The deer that ye hae hunted lang,
   Is seen ^ainto the Waste this day."   ^a *in*

" Then Hobie Noble is that deer;
   I wat he carries the style fu' ^ahie;   ^a *high*
Aft has he beat you ^bslough-hounds back,   ^b *sleuth-hounds*
   And set yourselves at little ^cee. . . ."   ^c *awe*

But Hobie Noble is betrayed—and by an Armstrong, Sim o' the Mains, one of the clan with whom he had leagued, and those others he had thought his " feres " (friends) :

There was heaps of men now Hobie before,
   And other heaps was him behind,
That had he been as ^awight as Wallace was   ^a *strong, active*
   Away brave Noble he could not win.

The Hobie he had but a laddie's sword,
   But he did more than a laddie's deed;
In the midst of Conscouthart Green,
   He brak it ower Jers a Wigham's ^aheid.   ^a *head*

Now they have ^ataen brave Hobie Noble,   ^a *taken*
   Wi his ain bowstring they ^bband him sae;   ^b *bound*
And I wat his heart was ne'er sae ^csair   ^c *sore*
   As then his ain five band him on the brae.

They have taen him on for West Carlisle;
   They ask'd him if he knew the way;
Whate'er he thought, yet little he said;
   He knew the way as well as they. . . .

Nothing arouses the wrath of a true Borderer more than a betrayal, the breaking of a bond, and tradition says the Laird of Mangerton, Chief of the Armstrongs, was swift to bring retribution on the degenerate member of his house, Sim o' the Mains. The ballad is a long one, full of the rhythmic repetition and the dramatic tension of alternating hope and despair that is so strong in the ballad. The characters, too, are drawn with an uncanny skill :

They hae taen him up the Ricker-gate;
   The wives they cast their windows wide;
And ^ailka wife to anither ^bcan say,   ^a *every* ^b *did*
   " That's the man loos'd Jock o the Side! "

" Fy on ye women! Why ca' ye me man?
　For it's nae man that I'm us'd like;
I'am but like a ᵃforfochen hound,　　　　ᵃ *exhausted*
　Has been fighting in a dirty ᵇsyke. . . .　ᵇ *field drain*

" Now fare thee well, sweet Mangerton!
　For I think again I'll ne'er thee see;
I wad betray nae lad alive,
　For a' the ᵃgowd in Christentie. . . .　ᵃ *gold*

" Yet I'd rather be ca'd Hobie Noble,
　In Carlisle, where he suffers for his ᵃfaut,　ᵃ *fault*
Before I were ca'd traitor Mains,
　That eats and drinks of meal and ᵇmaut."　ᵇ *malt*

There seems little difference between the Scots and the English
Borderer!

I was standing now, I knew, on the edge of the " Debatable
Lands"; further on was Tarras Moss, the hiding-place of the outlaws
and those mosstroopers pursued by the English warden after a raid.
It was said to be impassable on foot, but the Border ponies could
always pick their way. Tradition tells how after Carlanrig one of
the King's men, on reaching the castle, mounted one of Armstrong's horses, which bolted immediately, could not be stopped,
and took its rider straight to Tarras Moss, and into the avenging
arms of the sole survivor of Johnie's band!

One has to stand on a bleak hillside, perhaps shivering a little as
I was beginning to do in the caller air and the excitement of the
occasion, to fully sense the atmosphere of this wild Debatable
Land. I ranged the hills with my field-glasses. It was all eerily
beautiful—the mists rising and falling over a welter of hills, the sun
making a rift here and there, so that a hollow would be filled to the
brim with golden light while others remained dark and impene-
trable.

Some of the other watchers on the hillside with more powerful
binoculars than mine, and with expert knowledge of the course,
which is ten miles long, seemed to be beginning to pick out the
returning pack on the opposite hillside. Now they had disappeared
in a hollow; now they were breasting the crest of the field, now
they were racing across to the finishing line, each dog urged to a
desperate last spurt by the whistles and flagging-down of his
master. Excited commotion on the hillside reached fever pitch,
the watchers seeming to know every dog on sight.

I am told it was one of the most exciting finishes for years—three leading dogs separated by about a tail's length, with a few others not far behind. The rest continued to come in gallantly, but some of them were very " forfochen " hounds! A Walton (Cumberland) dog won the cup—the " blue riband " of the Border hound trails, which are popular on the English side, but do not appear at any other Scottish Common Riding.

I have seen all the older Common Ridings and found them all different in some respect. They are alike in that they commemorate the perambulation of the common lands. But they have all evolved and now incorporate some incident particular to their locality. Selkirk and Hawick recall Flodden: Selkirk the " fatal field " and the return of the lone horseman bearing a flag—it is a lament for the " Flo'ers o' the Forest a' wede away," embodying all the poetry and pathos of the Cymri; Hawick, an incident *after* Flodden, when a band of youths went out from the town to intercept a marauding party of English soldiers, and returned with a captured flag—it is a triumphant paean. Lauder was based on a religious ceremony, Peebles on a pagan festival. In what way, I wondered, would Langholm be different?

In 1816, after Beattie's death, Archie Thomson with John Irving and Frank Beattie, decided to ride instead of walk the round and afterwards they raced their horses on the Kilngreen. The number of riders increased yearly (as I have remarked elsewhere, the Borderer seizes every excuse to mount a horse) and a leader, or Cornet, was chosen.

At 8.30 a.m. in the square the horses took over. I was alone in the packed crowd. I had chosen not to have a guide. I was an outsider and I wanted to get an outsider's impression. I have not had the good fortune to be born or brought up in a Common Riding burgh.

Beside me were two fair-haired Scandinavians, who were evidently having the ritual explained to them. They could well be descendants of the first invading Norsemen, who had left their mark in so many place-names, and their influence in some of the ballad sagas.

What struck me first about the crowd was that, although Langholm is a mill town, it was a predominantly rural one. There was no mistaking these men with their lean bodies, weathered faces and loping shepherd's stride. Many of the farmers would already be mounted to follow the Cornet—not that the riders are confined to men: many women, and some young children, were also in the Cornet's cavalcade.

The trouble with these Common Ridings is that so much takes place in different spots and unless you know the ropes and are quick on your feet you are bound to miss some part. I decided to stay with the crowd in the Market Place, so I saw the Cornet arrive with more than a hundred followers, escorted by the town band to receive the Burgh Flag from the Provost; the procession carrying the emblems (a giant Thistle, Spade, Saut Herring and Barley Bannock nailed to a round platter by a " twal-penny nail " and a Floral Crown); the children carrying their " heather besoms " and clutching their new threepenny bits; and the first and third Crying of The Fair. But I should have been with the equally large crowd on Whita to see the riders take the hill to the Castle Craigs, where the second crying of the Fair takes place and the traditional barley bannocks and saut herrings are served, and afterwards witness the hazardous descent.

It is all traditional symbolism of course: the giant Thistle is the Scottish emblem; the Spade was for clearing the ditches and cutting the sod at the various boundaries; the Barley Bannock was one of the perquisites of the servant of baronial mill, while the twal-penny nail was used to nail an offender's ear to the Tron; the Saut Herring may have had something to do with the jealously-held fishing rights, or simply be " kitchen " (the old Scots word for relish); the Floral Crown may just be an added gaiety.

But there is always the something more that only a poet can convey, and I think Dr Christopher Grieve (" Hugh MacDiarmid "), Langholm's most distinguished native, has done it:

Drums in the Walligate, pipes in the air,
Come and hear the *a*cryin' o' the Fair.   *a proclaiming*

A' as it used to be, when I was a *a*loon   *a boy*
On Common-Ridin' Day in the Muckle Toon.

The bearer twirls the Bannock-and-Saut-
    Herrin',
The Croon o' Roses through the lift is farin',

The *a*auch-fit thistle wallops on *b*hie;   *a 8-ft.* *b high*
In heather besoms a' the hills gang by.

But noo it's a' the fish o' the sea
Nailed on the roond o' the Earth to me.

Beauty and Love that are bobbin' there;
Syne the ªbreengin' growth that alane I bear;   ª *bursting*

And Scotland followin' on ahint
For threepenny bits spleet-new frae the mint.

Drums in the Walligate, pipes in the air. . . .

I think one of the most entrancing sights I have ever seen was these children with their heather besoms mingled with wild flowers—all Scotland and the heather hills going by. No doubt the smallest thought of little else than their new threepenny bits, but I warrant there were some boys there who envisaged the day they might be the Cornet on their Common Riding day—the roond o' the Earth to them.

But, standing as I was literally and metaphorically on the fringe of the crowd, it was the crying of the Fair that intrigued me. Close as Langholm is to the Border line, long as their history of feud and foray, it was none of these things they were commemorating.

John Elliot was crying the Fair for the twenty-eighth time. He climbed up behind one of the riders on the broad back of a horse to do it. The horse stood where the Cross had been. It is quite a circus act, and carried out in this instance by a born clown, I didn't know which to admire most the iron control of the horseman, the complete immobility of the mount, or the equilibrium of the Town Crier while delivering every word with great gusto and appropriate dramatic gestures: this first part is not the original crying of the fair, but refers to the Common Riding.

Seelance!

This is the Proclamation of the Langholm Fair and Common Riding held the day after the Simmer or Lamb Fair in July annually.

Gentlemen—the first thing that Aw'm gan tae acquaint ye wi' are the names of the Portioner's Gruns o' Langholm, and from whence their services are from— [Then comes the inevitable rhyme, for the Borderer will rhyme as readily as mount a horse.]

Now Gentlemen we're gain frae the Toun,
And first of a' the Kiln-Green we gang roon';
It is an ancient place where clay is got,

And it belangs tae us by Right and Lot,
And then frae there the Lang-wood we gang throu'
Where everyane may breckons cut and pu',
And last of a' we to the Moss do steer,
To see gif a' oor Marches they be clear,
And when unto the Castle Craigs we come,
Aw'll cry the Langholm Fair and then we'll beat the drum.

Now gentlemen what ye have heard this day concerning gangin' roon' oor Marches, it is expected that every yin who has occasion for Peats, Breckons, Flacks, Stanes or Clay, will gang oot in defence o' their property, and they shall hear the Proclamation o' the Langholm Fair upon the Castle Craigs.

This was the signal for the Cornet and his followers to dash up the Kirk Wynd, the Cornet having to hold the flag with one hand and control his horse with the other! It needs the old moss-trooper's skill, with knee as well as hand.

When the horsemen returned from the hill, joined by the rest of the procession, the Common Riding motive was recounted again in verse: the Fair was again cried.

What followed is the real ancient Proclamation, if now corrupted, like all oral traditions:

Hoys, Yes! That's ae time! Hoys, Yes! That's
Twae times! Hoys, Yes! That's the third and last time!

This is tae gi'e notice!

That there's a muckle Fair to be hadden in the Muckle Toon o' the Langholm, on the 15th day of July, auld style, upon His Grace the Duke o' Buccleuch's Merk Land, for the space o' eight days and upwards; and a' land-loupers, and dub-scoupers, and gae-by-the-gate swingers, that come here tae breed hurdums or durdums, huliments or buliments, hagglements or bragglements, or tae molest this public Fair, they shall be ta'en by order o' the Baillie an' the Toon Cooncil, and their lugs shall be nailed tae the Tron wi' a twal-penny nail; and they shall sit doon on their bare knees and pray seeven times for the King, thrice for the Muckle Laird o' Ralton, and pay a groat tae mee, Jamie Ferguson, Baillie o' the aforesaid Manor, and Aw'll away hame an' hae a barley banna' an' a saut herrin' tae my denner by way o' auld style.

Huzza! Huzza! Huzza!

The town crier and the crowd had been thoroughly enjoying themselves. The oration had been punctuated by laughter and now there was hearty applause. Suddenly I felt I knew what they were commemorating—the spirit of sturdy independence of the old burghers and the irrepressible humour of the Scottish Borderer. The procession wheeled about and made for the Kilngreen, where the last sods are cut; the Esk is forded to the Castleholm, and the Cornet's Chase and the races and games are held. Some of the races are still traditionally confined to mounts that have gone round the marches, and the most popular entry for the games seems to be the wrestling, which is carried out " under Cumberland and Westmorland Association Rules."

By five o'clock the afternoon's heavy showers cleared to a brilliant evening. The " shows " on the Kilngreen were warming up. The flag was to be returned in the square at 9.15 p.m., and in the interval I decided to climb Whita, 1,162 ft., to the " Monument," the turning point of the Ride.

I took the hoof-prints, still fresh, as my guide and marvelled at the skill of both horse and rider that could cover such ground. This was no place for dude riders. They were of the old moss-trooper breed. This was the country of the Armstrongs and Elliots, the wildest of all the wild Border clans, more often than not together in a foray:

> Armstrongs and Elliots
> Ride theivis all.

There had been Armstrongs and Elliots in the Riding today:

> Armstrongs and Elliots! And how should they forget
> The pride their fathers gathered round the roving
>   reckless names?
> Can't you hear the horses neighing, and the riders
>   jesting yet? . . .

our modern balladist, Will Ogilvie, has written.

It was a calm clear evening, so very still it seemed after the rousing day. Down in Langholm they were still celebrating. I could see the Solway, faintly silver, and beyond the Westmorland hills. Below, to the south-west, lay the flat, fat Cumberland plain, and Scots Dyke that marks the Border line. I could follow it mentally through these Liddesdale wilds to the Cheviots and down again to the quiet pastoral reaches of lower Tweed to the sea. What a land of contrasts! And what a history! Along its length were the standing stones and stone circles of a prehistoric people who were there " before the siege of Troy "; the hill forts and settlements of the ancient Britons; the Roman roads and camps; the medieval towers. It had been the battleground of pagan and Christian, Picts and Romans, Celts and Angles, Norsemen, Scots and English. It had hardly ever known respite from fire or sword in all its recorded history until a Scottish king came to the throne of England. It bred a hardy race of men, of which the moss-trooper, freebooter, reiver—as he was variously dubbed—was the unique product. A weaker type would have been submerged or become servile. In the long Wars of Independence his land was in the path of every invading army, from whichever side, his crops trampled, his property put to the flames. Raiding became a profession, with an element of sport; and whoever had most in the larder could best stand a raid!

It also bred, curiously enough, a certain kinship between the peoples on both sides of the line. They were never " foreigners " to each other, as the Southerners and the Highlanders were " foreigners "—they were simply " over-the-fell men." And they remain so today; as I had just had proof in Langholm.

And it bred the Border balladists. Of the ballads Quiller Couch has stated: " They crowd thicker and thicker as on either side they near the ancient Border line of the two kingdoms," and G. M. Trevelyan has summed up: " Most of them, including many of the best, were written on the Scottish side, but some quite certainly in England, like Chevy Chase; and The Death of Percy Reid, Lambkin, The Fair Flower of Northumberland, and Fair Mary of Wallington, all tell of Northumberland tragedies."

So the Border line was, after all, a very artificial one. But for centuries the two kingdoms contended for it, Commission after Commission was sent to " settle " the line, one strip of land becoming for a time the disputed, or " debatable," land—a kind of no-man's-land.

James VI, perhaps the least loved of the Stuart kings, but for whom I hope to have a good word to say, when he came to his English inheritance was determined not only to put an end to the Border feuds and forays once and for all (something his predecessors had tried and failed to do) but to wipe out the entire Border line. The Border counties were to become his " middle shires."

He did accomplish the suppression of the reivers by means so ruthless that he left a long-lingering hatred in Liddesdale, especially among the Grahams. But he never succeeded in erasing the line. Geographically it remains much as it was finally defined in the sixteenth century, something in which the people on both sides take a kind of proprietary pride.

When I came down to the square again it was filling up and by 9.15 it was jammed, in spite of the counter-attraction of the " shows." When the Cornet arrived to hand back the flag he could hardly manoeuvre his horse towards the dais. There was a sudden tenseness in the crowd that I had not sensed before. This was the final, the supreme act of the day. It was no play acting, no mere pageant. Their chosen man had carried their Burgh Flag worthily all day. Ask any Cornet, and he will tell you that this was the proudest day of his life, and he will mean it.

Now he had handed back the flag—handed back his brief moment of glory.

The Town Band struck up " Auld Lang Syne." The crowd joined hands and sang. And on that note the Langholm Common Riding closed.

II

The Armstrong Story

LANGHOLM STRADDLES the main road to Carlisle, which crosses the Border line at Scots Dyke. I was still on the trail of Johnie Armstrong of Gilnockie, but it was going to be difficult to find traces of him and his clan. There were, I was told, no Armstrongs now owning land in a country where they had been paramount. Once their towers had been thick in the Debatable Land and in Liddesdale and up Ewes Valley. Their chief, whose stronghold was Mangerton Tower, could summon 3,000 men at call, and Wheathaugh was scarcely less powerful. Johnie of Gilnockie was the acknowledged leader.

I could have taken the direct way to " Gilnockie " (or Hollows) Tower by the main road from which it is clearly seen and easily approached, about midway between Langholm and Canonbie.

But I chose the quieter way which would cross the Tarras Water, on the boundary line of the Debatable Land.

The road branched left at the Skipper's Bridge, about a mile out of the town, one of the lovely old stone bridges, still unspoiled by widening and the substitution of railings for the original stone parapets. Telford, as apprentice, worked on this bridge. " Deep in the saul the early scene," Lewis Spence has written, and Telford loved the Esk, near whose upper reaches he was born. It is indeed a beautiful stream, the current broken by large boulders and shelving rocks and " of such crystalline or colourless clearness, no other stream I have ever seen being comparable " as Pennant, the eighteenth-century traveller, declared. The banks too are here lightly wooded with scrub and hardwood trees which, in our stonier soil, seem to take on a deeper brilliance of autumn colouring than in the softer south. Spring is sometimes slow and reluctant in the Borders, but autumn correspondingly lingers longer, reaching its zenith of colouring in late October. Yet this is just the time when the average visitor has gone, and those who

[18]

associate Scotland only with the heather bloom do not know the glory of the autumn bracken on the hillsides and these tree-lined rivers.

The road followed the riverside to the woods at Broomholm. A Maxwell had lived at Broomholm until recently, and one of the ballads, first published in Scott's *Minstrelsy*, was written round the exiled Lord Maxwell—" Lord Maxwell's Last Goodnight."

These Maxwells were the same family who had given the name to Maxton village—the " tun " of Maccus, about midway between Melrose and Kelso, and to the famous salmon pool at Kelso and the haugh above. But they had gone west to become sheriffs of Dumfriesshire and Wardens of the Marches.

A Ewen de Maccuswell had been with Malcolm Canmore at the siege of Alnwick: by marrying a daughter of the Lord of Galloway he obtained Caerlaverock Castle, and round that castle and Threave much of the later history of the Maxwells revolves—of forfeiture, restoration, capture, imprisonment, escape, exile and execution. If Scotland is the " home of lost causes " the Maxwells were nearly always on the losing side.

The fourth Lord Maxwell fell at Flodden, the fifth lord was captured at Solway Moss. The Maxwells fought in the lost causes of Mary, Queen of Scots, Charles I, and the Pretender. Was it that Celtic strain which Renan describes: " whose very fidelity has been useless devotion . . . faithful to its conquerors when its conquerors are no longer faithful to themselves . . . in defence of desperate causes " ?

As hereditary Wardens of the West March they had a stormy passage, and it was rivalry over the Wardenship between the Johnstones and the Maxwells that led to the battle of Dryffe Sands and the subsequent exile of the young Maxwell chief.

The Wardenship was always a jealously-held honour: The Maxwells had long held the Wardenship until in 1578 Lord Maxwell was deposed allegedly " for notorious neglect of his duties " (probably Johnie Armstrong comes in here) and the Wardenship given to Johnstone.

The clash came at Dryfe Sands, in 1593 Maxwell lost 700 men and was most brutally mutilated and killed. His son vowed vengeance. The inevitable encounter followed—some say that it was a genuine attempt at a staunching of the "deadly feud," others that Johnstone was lured on that pretext. But the first shots are believed to have been fired by the adherents, not the principals, as so often happened in Border frays, and in the melee that ensued Maxwell shot Johnstone in the back. He had to flee to France. He was only thirty-two.

> The wind was fair, the ship was close—
> That good lord went away,
> And most part of his friends were there,
> To give him a fair convay . . .

A Maxwell of Broomholm and an Armstrong are said to have been among the friends who saw him embark. The Warden Maxwell has been suspected in some quarters of being implicated in the betrayal of Johnie at Carlanrig. He received much of Armstrong's land by royal decree, but he may only have been receiving what he had first given. The fact that the Armstrongs thereafter fought for Maxwell at Dryfe Sands seems to disprove the accusation.

This ballad has undoubted historical foundation. That of Johnie of Carlanrig rests chiefly on the tradition of the people and the testimony of an old historian—Lindsay of Pitscottie, which Lang dismisses as " late gossip "! The late Sir Herbert Maxwell comments somewhat acidly " it is just the sort of story that would gain currency and evidence in a district where half the contestants were Mosstroopers and the rest in league with them."

Yet no historical happening or any ballad, excepting Otterburn, has made a deeper impression on the countryside. That it was an event still very much alive in the people's memory seems proved by Sir David Lindsay of the Mount's reference to it in the *Thrie Estates*: " ane cord, baith great and lang quhilk hangit Johnie the Armistrang."

I recalled what my friend Mr Robin Lorimer had written in a letter: " Most of these Border ballads probably have the function of perpetuating a tradition that some particular family has produced in order to give its account of some important event. If one can find out how the family's interest affects its account of any such matter, it should finally be possible to discover just how the resultant ballad is related to the historical record of the event."

Some historians, I knew, had surmised that Pitscottie had either based his account of the hanging of Johnie Armstrong on the ballad then existing, or that the ballad had arisen from Pitscottie's account (*c.* 1550).

Mr Lorimer, however, made the point that " though there are many striking verbal coincidences between these two accounts, Pitscottie omits many equally striking details, and the order in which he arranges his material is quite different. Altogether, he tells the story so differently that it is difficult to suppose he can have taken his account directly from the ballad, or even from an earlier version of it. But it seems equally unlikely that the ballad can have been derived, directly or indirectly, from Pitscottie's account."

This I thought seemed logical. How, then, when it is not included in state papers, had Pitscottie come by his account? And how had the ballad itself originated?

" The Armstrongs must surely have had their own tradition-account of the matter," Mr Lorimer had thought. " And it is not unduly speculative to suppose that their account was probably first made up soon after the hanging; that it was originally in prose; and that each subsequent generation of Armstrongs continued to hand it down, perhaps still in prose in their local oral tradition. Allan Ramsay's version of the ballad, which he says was copied from the mouth of an Armstrong in the sixth generation from ' this John ' may originally have been derived from some such version of the story, perhaps in prose, preserved in the Armstrong family tradition; and Pitscottie's account may very well have had, at any rate in part, the same origin."

My thoughts had carried me up the steep hill from Broomholm to the open moorlike country, sparsely cultivated. In about a mile or so the road dipped again sharply to a deep ravine and bridge over Tarras Water.

Tarras is a rocky, turbulent stream, fit offspring of the wild Tarras Moss from which it springs higher up. Like Till, at the other end of the Border line, it has a sinister reputation.

I was looking for the " Fairy Lowp," but it seemed to be on the Byre Burn, which runs by a disused road. As the road climbed again and continued in open country there seemed many side roads but I pushed on through Gilnockie village and down to " Nell's Bridge," and there, sure enough the side road on the right was barricaded. " Road closed. Blocked with snow." a weathered board read, and a printed notice said that this road had ceased to be a road " within the meaning of the Act." Roads still on maps

c

have such a way of disappearing, or petering out to a track in the
wilderness, while new metalled roads appear where only tracks
were marked.

It will be a great pity if this quiet road falls into complete disuse.
It follows the Byre Burn till it falls into Esk. The burn is rather like
a smaller Tarras. A small but pretty linn, halfway, forms the
Fairy Lowp. The countryman has a way of turning over the loveliest bits to the fairies and the gentler happenings, and it is well to
remember that these occur as frequently as " Bloody Bushes " and
" Devil's Waters." Not all the tales of the Borders are of " old
unhappy far off things and battles long ago."

The quiet glen seemed all too short. I came out to the heavy
traffic of the Carlisle road. Turning right again, in a few minutes
I was at Gilnockie Bridge where, at the east end, local tradition
sites Johnie Armstrong's tower; and the *Ancient Monuments of
Dumfriesshire* places " a fort of the familiar type." No better site
could have been chosen for either fort or tower. The banks rise
precipitously from the Esk, the swift current foaming over great
boulders. Local tradition also asserts that the stones from the old
castle went into the building of the bridge—as probably did the
Priory stones into the Canonbie Bridge.

Many of the boulders in the bed of the stream looked to me as if
they had fallen there, and had been shaped more by hand than the
action of the water.

Hollows Mill stands at the west end of the bridge. Johnie
Armstrong had boasted of

> " Gude four and twenty ganging mills,
> That gang throw a' the yeir to me."

So I thought I would go by way of the mill along the banks of
the Esk to Hollows Tower, instead of continuing along the road.

From the road the tower looks a very ordinary one, though
compact and sturdy, needing only a roof to complete it. But seen
standing on a bluff above a beautiful bend of the river it takes on
something of the grace of its site. It is not such a defensive site as
that at Gilnockie Bridge, and the present building, antiquarians say,
is obviously of a later date than the time of John Armstrong. It
has an unusual corbelling not found on the older types, but one
gable is shaped to hold the bale fire, made compulsory by Act of

Parliament when the Defence of the Borders laws were codified—
a Maxwell being one of the Commissioners.

Why of all the Armstrong towers—and this one is in the heart of
the Debatable Land—was this one spared? The Armstrong story
is full of unanswered questions. Why did Johnie Armstrong go so
readily in response to James V's " luving letter " when not one
Armstrong had turned up when James IV summoned them to his
Justice Court at Dumfries? Why, too, is there no mention of the
hanging in the State Papers though they contain many accounts of
other hangings of notable Border chiefs?

I was given the keys and told I could climb to the top of the
tower. This might not be Johnie's actual tower but it was the last
standing link with the Armstrongs. And if you would get the full
flavour of the story, climb to the top of Hollows Tower, and with a
keen wind from Solway in your hair go over the whole of that
magnificent ballad of Johnie Armstrong.

Then take the road to Carlanrig, as I did on another day, and
trace step by step Johnie's progress to its tragic end.

Beyond Langholm Castle the Ewes Valley widens out with the
Ewes Water, a modest stream, winding through meadow-like land
with the high hills set well back like a great wall. A pleasant and
pastoral foreground, but beyond that wall lay the wildest tract in
the southern uplands, and in which even in Scott's day there were
no roads. It is a land of 2,000 feet hills and morasses.

Johnie Armstrong was still in his own domain:

> All between heir and Newcastle town
> Shall pay thair yeirly rent to thee

was the " brave gift " he offered the King.

It was no vain boast. The Armstrongs at that time possessed
large areas not only in the Debatable Land but in Ewesdale,
Eskdale, Wauchopedale, and Annandale. But with all their
power they had a reputation for lawlessness and depredations that
had called forth from the Bishop of Glasgow the famous " Moni-
tion of cursing."

James I had been the first of the Stuart Kings to vow he would
" make the rush bush keep the cow." James V was but following
the policy of his ancestors. But the fact was the Stuart Kings were
too remote from the Borders. They were little more than " the

Kings of Fife " to the Borderer, and they had the misfortune to come to the throne either as minors, to be ruled in their formative years by powerful and ambitious nobles, or exiled to English or French courts, and they were often ill-advised by their counsellers.

There seems some reason in believing that James V was not solely to blame for the betrayal of Johnie. But one would have thought that the " Gaberlunzie King," confrère of gypsies, would have had more sympathy for the reivers. Was all mention of the episode omitted from the State Papers because James V was ashamed of it—as on smaller scale the minister of Wauchope omitted from his statistical account the Roman bridge, for the destruction of which he was held responsible?

If the Ewes Valley looked as pleasant that July day in 1529 when Johnie and his " gallant companie " passed through as it did to me today, I thought, he would be in ebullient mood. He was as much king here as James V was in Fife.

> When Johnie came before the king,
>   With all his men sae brave to see
> The king he movit his bonnet to him;
>   He ween'd he was a king as well as he.

Pitscottie says: " when the King saw him and his men so gorgeous in their apparel and so many braw men under a tyrant's commandment, thowardlie he turned about face and bade take that tyrant out of his sight, saying, ' What wants yon knave that a king should have? ' "

As the ballad has it, when Johnie pleads for the life of himself and his men in exchange for rich ransoms:

> " Away, away, thou traitor strang!
>   Out of my sicht thou may'st sune be.
> I grantit never a traitor's life,
>   And now I'll not begin with thee."

> " Ye lied, ye lied, now, king ", he says,
>   " Althocht a king and prince ye be,
> For I ᵃluid naething in all my life   ᵃ *loved*
>   I dare well say it, but honesty;

> " But a fat horse, and a fair woman,
>   Twa bonny dogs to kill a deir;

But England and ^asuld hav' found me ^bmeil and   *a should*   *b meal*
    ^cmaut,   *c malt*
    ^dGif I had liv'd this hundred yeir! ...   *d if*

" To seik ^ahet water beneth cauld ice,   *a hot*
    Surely it is great follie;
I hae asked grace of a graceless face,
    But there is nane for my men and me.

" But had I kend ^aor I came frae hame,   *a ere*
    How thou ^bunkynd wadst been to me,   *b inhuman*
I wad haif kept the border-side
    In spite o' all thy force and thee." ...

Tradition says that it was at a spot, near Fiddleton Toll, where the Ewes Valley ends in a narrow pass and the hills pile up menacingly, the king encamped, still called Camp Knowe. The Armstrongs were said to be unarmed when they were ambushed by the Frostlee Burn. This seems likely, as otherwise they would certainly have put up a fight.

" Efter this hunting," says Pitscottie, " the king hangit Johnie Armstrang Laird of Gilnockie, quhilk monie Scottish men heavily lamented, for he was ane doubit man and also guid a chieftain as ever was on the borderis of Scotlande or England." And, in the words of the ballad:

John murdred was at Carlinrigg,
    And all his gallant companie;
But Scotland's heart was never sae wae
    To see sae mony brave men die—

Because they sav'd their country ^adeir   *a dear*
    Frae Englishmen: Nane were sae ^bbauld   *b bold*
While Johnie lived on the Border side
    Nane o' them daurst cum neir his ^chauld.   *c hold*

In Carlanrig Kirkyard I found the tablet bearing the crest of the " Strong Arm," commemorating the tradition. The date is given as 1530.

Dates may differ, the tradition varies little. Now I had heard that the country people declared the very trees on which the men were hanged withered away with the blackness of the deed; and at Carlanrig Farmhouse, this is the story I was told:

" John Armstrong when he was hung was only in his forties.

The tradition is that the trees on which he and his men were hung died, and it was said in the country that no trees would ever grow there again to reach the age of Johnie. My Grannie laughed at the superstition and planted trees for a shelter foundation for the farmhouse, but while they were still young they were all blown down in a gale. She said it was just coincidence and made another planting, and again the trees were blown down while still young."

The winds can blow strongly round that elevated and lonely farmhouse. But the people's sense of moral justice—so strong in folk lore—was satisfied that even the very trees should die.

Canonbie seemed the best base from which to explore the Debatable Land—of which it had been the centre—and continue the Armstrong story.

I did not propose to seek out the sites of all those towers which had continued to go up in face of the decree issued by the Earl of Cumberland and Lord Maxwell that no new building was to be carried out in the Debatable Land, though all might pasture their stock by day within its bounds provided they were removed by night. This was intended to stop raiding. But the Armstrongs considered it their particular territory. Raid and counter-raid went on. Lord Dacre brought up a force of 2,000 men against them and was defeated, but he had managed to burn Hole-hous (Hollows). The Armstrongs the very same day followed and burned Netherby. This put both Wardens in a fix. Dacre claimed damages for Netherby, Maxwell for Hollows. Dacre's last word was that Hollows was not in Eskdale but in the Debatable Land over which Maxwell had no jurisdiction.

But I particularly wished to find the sites, or near-sites, of other Armstrong ballads—" Jock o' the Syde," and " Dick o' the Cow."

These redoubtable characters were well known as far as the Lammermuirs. Maitland of Lethington in his " complaynt " gives a good idea of their depredations and their " to-names " (nicknames) which were necessary to distinguish individuals of a clan all of one surname. He also gives lists of " insight," the gear of a house " lifted " in addition to stock. It is a valuable commentary on the life and living conditions of the people, but too long to quote in full.

Of Liddesdale the common theivis
    Sae pertlie ^asteilis now and ^breivis   ^a *steal*   ^b *plunder*
That nane may keip
    Horse, ^cnowt, nor scheip   ^c *cattle*
Nor yet daur sleip
    For their mischeifis. . . .

    Yet, ^aor I die,   ^a *before*
Sum sall thame see
    ^bHing on a tree   ^b *hang*
^cQuhill thay be ^ddeid.   ^c *until*   ^d *dead*

The country was not particularly attractive after climbing out of the Esk Valley from Canonbie, but the road becomes more interesting with increasing glimpses of the Liddel Water which forms the Border line from Esk to Kershopefoot. At one point the road crosses the Mere (March) Burn which runs into the Liddel at Liddelbank. This is the first point on the Border line where the two countries and three counties meet (Dumfriesshire, Cumberland and Roxburghshire).

The Mere Burn rises in the very apex of the Debatable Land, which does not, as some think, include all wild Liddesdale. It was only a tract of some 10 by $3\frac{1}{2}$ miles and included a good bit of level land which is now in Cumberland. It contained most of the parish of Canonbie and Morton and all of Kirkandrews.

As " debatable land " it seems first to have been mentioned in 1450, when Cumbria claimed it. In 1493 Henry VII sent a Commission which failed to decide anything. In 1543 Henry VIII claimed Canonbie Priory, but did not succeed in getting it. In 1550 both English and Scottish Wardens claimed possession of the whole area. But at no time did the Scots even admit that it was " debatable." Canonbie Priory was attached to Jed Abbey.

In the year 1551 the Debatable Land had become largely the refuge of " broken men," those who had no recognised chief to stand surety for them, and notable outlaws " put to the horn." A proclamation went forth to clear the Debatable Land, which exceeded in ferocity anything the reivers had ever done. All Englishmen and Scotsmen were to be " free to rob, burn, spoil, slay, murder, or destroy all and every such person or persons, their bodies, buildings, goods and cattle, as do or shall remain or shall inhabit upon any part of the said Debatable Land, without any redress to be made to the same."

Finally in 1552 the Commissioners appointed by both kingdoms really got down to " settling " the Border line " so that ilk realme might ken their awn part and puniss the inhabitants thereof for their demerits," to which the Scots agreed " providing alwayes that Canonbye fall hail to Scotland." The emphasis was always on the punishment, of a race that, through sheer desperate straits had become—in Maitland's eyes—" common theivis "; but, with more justice, a hardy and independent race with a rough chivalry and high humour, ruthless on occasion but again with a surprising gentleness and compassion, as the ballads tell.

At Underburnmouth two men were about to set off to spend their Saturday afternoon fishing in the Liddel.

" Which is the way, please, to Red Moss? " I asked.

" Up there," they replied in unison, pointing to the signpost which said " Tinnis Farm."

" And where is Syde? "

" It's up there, too," I was told. " But there is nothing to be seen now."

" Yes . . ." I said ". . . I know."

What, I asked myself as I took the hill road, had I come out to see? What could I hope to find there?—Nothing but what the imagination could call up from an empty site. And, chiefly, I suppose, I was there because the very emptiness of the landscape appeals. To tramp the moorland wastes, to breathe the moorland air, to let the uncluttered imagination range free—that is enough for me.

Higher up I turned and looked back over the Liddel Valley rising beyond to the Bewcastle Fells, and the further blue, broken mass of Northumberland. In front the deepening red of the bracken, the tawny moorland grasses laid great swathes of colour over Red Moss.

To my left was Tinnis Hill (1,826 ft.) and Windy Edge, where prehistoric standing stones and cairns tell of the first peoples here. A side road led me down to Tinnis Burn in a narrow deep glen. Hereabouts would I find the site of the hamlet of " Syde " and the Armstrong tower of Puddingburn.

There was a bridge over the burn and beyond it the road climbed sharply and disappeared out of sight. A Border burn has almost a hypnotic effect on me. Others may be held by its music—for me it is the visual rhythm of the ebb and flow, the fall and eddy over and around rocks; it is the very essence of the repetitive rhythm of the ballad.

Dick o' the Cow would cross here: these bridges mark the old fords. I could see him pushing up that steep incline on the other side, fearful but determined; reaching the Armstrong tower over the ridge. The Armstrongs are meeting him and barring his way; he is being led into the hall. The trestles are set out on the rush-strewn floor, the boards are laid on them and the meal is set out. This is no " dish of spurs " to hint that the larder is empty and the clan must " ride," but a generous portion of Dickie's own cow. The aged minstrel is ensconced in the ingleside ready to chant some old ballad recounting the exploit of the clan, or gather material for a new one—his reward to be the whole, or part, of a stolen cow.

Perhaps he would be the one to give the first version of " Dick o' the Cow," said to be popular on both sides of the Border, for the Scottish Borderers could appreciate a jest against themselves— whether subsequently they sought reprisal or not.

The ballad tells that " fair Johnie Armstrong " (not Gilnockie) and " Willie " decided it was time to go after a little " bootie " at Hutton Hall. Over the border they find " the laird he was the wiser man, for he had left nae gear without." Says Johnie:

> " But how ca'd they the man we last met,
>   Billie, as we came ower the *a*knowe? "   *a knoll*
> " That same he is an innocent fool
>   And some men ca' him Dick o' the Cow."

> " That fool has three as good *a*kye of his own   *a cows*
>   As is in a' Cumberland, billie," quo' he:
> " Betide me life, betide me death,
>   These three kye sall go to Liddisdale with
>   me."

> Then they're com'd on to the poor fool's house,
>   And they have broken his wa's sae wide
> That they have loos'd out Dick o' the Cow's kye
>   three
> And ta'en three coverlets aff his wife's bed.

In the morning there is a great outcry from Dickie's gude wife:

> *a*" Haud thy tongue, my wife," he says,   *a hold*
>   " And of thy crying let me be,

And *b*aye that where thou wants a cow,   *b* *always*
   In gude *c*suth I'll bring thee three."   *c* *truth*

He goes first to Lord Scrope, the English Warden, whose jester
he seems to have been, and threatens to leave his service unless he
gets leave to go into Liddesdale to steal. He gets leave on condi-
tion that he swears he will steal from none but those who stole
from him, which he does. How Dickie, the fool, outwitted the
Armstrongs and got much, much more than his own back without
breaking his oath, is the essence of the jest.

He mounts and rides and he reaches Puddingburn:

    Yet he's com'd up to the ha' amang them a';
      Sae weil's he became his courtesie:
    " Weil may ye be, my gude Laird's Jock,
      But the Deil bless all your companie! "

Thus he addresses the Laird, and then he puts his complaint.
Fair Johnie and Willie threaten to hang him, another suggests a
beating and letting him go, but the Laird, while unable to resist a
dig at the English Borderer, is more merciful:

    Then up and spak the gude Laird's Jock,
      The best *a*falla in the companie: *a* *fellow*
    " *b*Fitt thy way doun a little while, Dickie,   *b* *foot*
      And a peice of thine own cow's *b*hoch I'll give   *c* *thigh*
        to thee."

Naturally the very thought sickens Dickie, but the other men make
haste to the feast, for

    Then it was the use of Puddinburn
      And the house of Mangerton, all hail!
    These that cam' not at the first ca'
      They gat nae mair till the next meal.

Dickie retires to brood over his wrongs. But the men in their
haste have thrown the stable key above the door and Dickie has
taken note. He ties the horses with " St Mary's knot," all except
three. One he mounts, one he leads, but the third is the Laird's
Jock's, which is left free in gratitude—or foresight!

On the morn, when they discover their loss, there is a great outcry from the Armstrongs and the Laird demands " What's that theif? " Fair Johnie laments:

> " Dick o' the Cow has been in the stable this
>   last nicht,
> And has ta'en my brither's horse and mine
>   frae me."

The Laird tells them they have got what they deserved:

> " Have ye not found my tales fu' ^aleal?   ^alit. *loyal*
> Ye wad never out of England bide,
>   Till crooked and blind and a' wad steal."

But after much pleading he agrees to lend Johnie the only free horse—his own.

> " He's baith worth gound and gude money;
> Dick o' the Cow has away twa horse,
>   I wishna thou ^asuldna make him three."   ^a *shouldn't*

Fair Johnie overtakes Dickie " hand for hand on Canobie Lee."

After making sure Johnie is alone Dickie reads him a sermon on his conduct:

> " There is a preacher in our chapel,
>   And a' the lee-lang day teaches he;
> When day is gane, and nicht is come,
>   There's never a word I mark but three.
>
> " The first and second's Faith and Conscience;
>   The Third is, Johnie, take heed of thee;
> But what faith and conscience had thou, traitor,
>   When thou took my three kye frae me? "

and, what is more,

> " Sent thy billie Willie ower the knowe,
>   And he took three coverlets aff my wife's
>   bed? "
> Then Johnie let a spear fa' ^alaich by his thigh,   ^a *low*

Thocht weil to run the innocent through;
But the Powers above was mair than he's,
He ran but the poor fool's jerkin through.

They became locked in combat and Dickie cannot " win at him
with the blade of the sword " but fells him with the pommel:

" Gramercie," then *a*can Dickie say,   *a did*
" I had twa horse, thou has made me three."

He takes the steel jack, cap and sword from the unconscious man
to show Lord Scrope.
When Johnie comes to, he exclaims:

" For if I suld live this hundred year,
I shall never *a*fecht with a fool after thee."   *a fight*

Dickie speeds to his master, but rumour has been swifter and
Lord Scrope threatens to hang him for breaking his oath. Dickie
answers with spirit:

" The shame speed the liars, my lord! " quo'
   Dickie,
" That was no the promise ye made to me;
For I'd never gane to Liddesdale to steal
   Till that I socht my leave at thee."

" But what *a*gart thou steal the Laird's Jock's *a made you*
   horse?
And, *b*limmer, what gart thou steal him? " *b rascal*
   quo' he;
" For lang *c*micht thou in Cumberland dwelt *c micht . . . have*
   *d*Or the Laird's Jock had *e*stown *f*ocht frae *d ere e stolen f aught*
   thee."

" Indeed I wat ye lied, my lord,
   And even so loud as I hear ye lie.
I wan him frae his man Fair Johnie Armstrong,
   Hand for hand on Canobie Lee.

" There's the *a*jack was on his back, *a coat of mail*
   The two-handed sword, that hung laich by
      his thigh;
There's the steel cap was on his heid;
   I have a' these tokens to let you see."

Lord Scrope then tries to strike a bargain. He will give Dickie £20 and one of his best cows, for the horse. Dickie is astute:

> *a*" Trow ye *b*aye to make a fule of me?   *a believe* *b always*
> I'll either have thirty pound for the gude horse,
> Or else *c*he's gae to Martan fair wi' me."   *c he'll go*

He gets his price and proceeds to Carlisle with the remaining two horses. He meets Lord Scrope's brother, who offers him £15 for " fair Johnie's horse " and gets the same reply. Dickie gets his second £30 and another good " milk-kye." And Dickie has the last laugh.

> " I wish the neck o' the third horse were broken,
> For I have a better of may ain, and ony better
>   can be."

And so, having sold the horses of the fair Johnie and his brother he rides home on the Laird's Jock's own " best bay " to his wife and:

> Judge ye how the poor fule he sped—
> He has given her three score English pounds
>   For the three auld co'erlets was ta'en aff her
>   bed,

and, besides, " twa as gude kye as all my three might be."

" There is nothing to see now." The once prosperous hamlet of Syde is one of these vanished settlements buried under the green turf of many a hillside. " Jock o' the Side " was cousin to the " Laird's Jock." He was lodged in Newcastle jail as usual as the consequence of a raid. His mother, Lady Downie, appeals to her brother, at Mangerton. No chief would refuse succour to a member of his clan—a Celtic trait for the clan was only an extension of the family.

He promises to send three of his trustiest men:

> " The Laird's Jock ane, the Laird's Wat twa,
>   Oh, Hobie Noble, thou ane *a*maun be;   *a must*
> Thy coat is blue, thou has been true,
>   Since England banish'd thee, to me."

He instructs them to shoe their horses the wrong way to confuse pursuers, and to dress to look like " corn-gangers gawn ae road." They make for the head waters of Tyne, and on to Chollerford. Here they cut a tree with " fifteen naggs upo ilk side " to serve as a scaling ladder, but it proves too short for the town walls.

The Laird's Jock says they must force the gates, but they are challenged by " a proud porter ", whom they overcome:

> Nou soon they reach Newcastle jail,
>   And to the pris'ner thus they call;
> " Sleeps thou, wauks thou, Jock o' the Side?
>   Or is thou wearied o' thy thrall? " . . .
>
> " Aft, aft I wauk, I seldom sleep;
>   But wha's this kens my name sae weil? " . . .
>
> Then up and spak the gude Laird's Jock,
>   " Ne'er fear ye nou, my billie," quo' he;
> " For here's the Laird's Jock, the Laird's Wat,
>   And Hobie Noble, come to set thee free."
>
> " Oh, *a*haud thy tongue, and speak nae mair,   *a* hold
>   And o' thy talk nou let me be!
> For if a' Liddesdale were here the nicht,
>   The morn's the day that I *b*maun die.   *b* must
>
> " Full fifteen *a*stane o' Spanish iron   *a* stone
>   They hae laid a' richt sair on me;
> Wi' locks and keys I am fast bound
>   Into this dungeon mirk and drearie."
>
> " Fear ye no that," quo' the Laird's Jock;
>   " A faint heart ne'er wan a fair ladie;
> Work thou within, we'll work without,
>   And I'll be bound we set thee free."

First and second doors go down in splinters under the " strong arm " and

> The pris'ner nou upo' his back
>   The Laird's Jock's gotten up fu' *a*hie;   *a* high
> And doun the stair him, irons and a',
>   Wi' nae sma' speed and joy brings he.
>
> " Nou Jock, I wat," quo' Hobie Noble,
>   " Part o' the *a*wecht ye may lay on me ";   *a* weight

" I wat weil no," quo' the Laird's Jock,
  " I count him lichter than a *b*flie."   *b fly* (pron. *flee*)

Sae out at the gates they a' are gane,
  The pris'ner's set on horseback *a*hie;   *a high*
And nou wi' speed they've ta'en the *b*gate,   *b road*
  While ilk ane jokes fu wantonlie.

Even in moments of extreme danger the Scots reiver must have his joke:

" O Jock, sae winsomely's ye ride,
  Wi' baith your feet upo' ae side,
Sae weil's ye're harness'd, and sae *a*trig,   *a neat*
  In troth ye sit like ony bride! "

The nicht, tho' wat, they didna mind,
  But hied them on fu' mirrilie,
Until then cam to Chollerford brae,
  Where the water ran like mountains hie.

They question an old man if he thinks the water will " ride." He replies: " I wat weil no." He had never seen the Tyne so big, not running " sae like the sea ":

Then up and spak the Laird's saft Wat,
  The greatest couard in the company;
" Now halt, now halt, we needna try't;
  The day is com'd we a' *a*maun die."   *a must*

" Poor fainthearted thief! " quo' the Laird's Jock,
  " There'll nae man die but he that's *a*fie;   *a fey, doomed*
I'll lead ye a' richt safely through;
  Lift ye the pris'ner on ahint me." ...

They scarce the ither side had won,
  When twenty men they saw pursue;
Frae Newcastle toun they had been sent
  A' English lads, richt gude and true.

But when the land-sergeant the water saw,
  " It winna ride, my lads," quo' he;
Then out he cries, " Ye the pris'ner may tak
  But leave the irons, I pray, to me! "

" I wat weil no," cried the Laird's Jock,
   " I'll keep them a', *a*shoon to my mare they'll   *a shoe*
       be;
My gude grey mare, for I am sure,
   She's bocht them a' fu' dear frae thee."

And so:

The pris'ner's brocht to his ain fireside. . . .

" Now Jock, my billie," quo' a' the three,
   " The day is com'd thou wast to die;
But thou's as weil at thy ain fireside,
   Nou sitting, I think, 'tween thee and me."

Bold, reckless, ruthless and cruel, audacious, loyal and merry
outlaws—these were the Armstrongs.

If James V had treated with Johnie of Gilnockie as James IV
did with the Outlaw Murray, the later history of the Armstrongs
might have been different. As it was, the day came when Maitland of Lethington's fervent wish was fulfilled with tragic finality.
There is a fragment of an old ballad set to a hauntingly beautiful
air, which—hearing it sung by an artless milkmaid—moved
Goldsmith to tears. It might well be taken for the epitaph of the
whole clan:

This night is my departing night
   For here nae longer must I stay;
There's neither friend nor foe of mine
   But wishes me away.

What I have done through lack of wit
   I never never can recall.
I hope ye're a' my friends as yet—
   Goodnight and joy be wi' ye all.

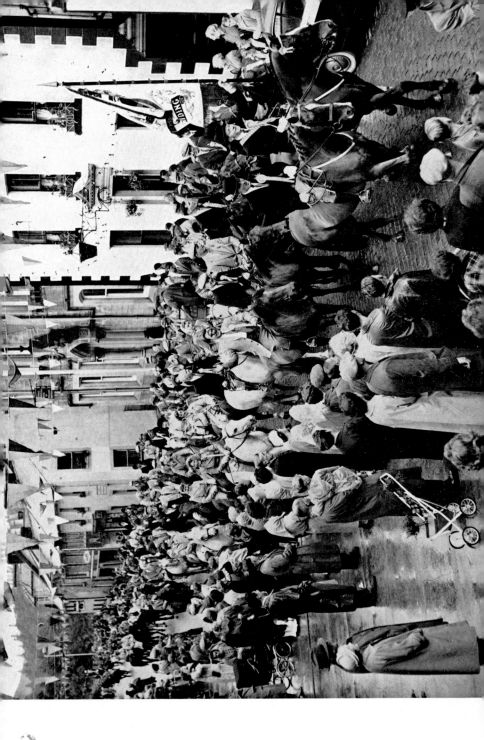

PLATE I
Langholm
Common
Riding

Photograph:
Cumberland
News

III

The Debatable Land

AMONG THOSE who followed Johnie of Gilnockie to Carlanrig was an Irvine of Stakeheuch. They were notable free-booters, Dick Irwen especially. The name is said to have over thirty different spellings. Irwin was the name by which they were known in Ulster (where many of the Borderers were deported, or voluntarily settled). An Irwin was one of the twelve apprentice boys who closed the gates of the city of Derry in the face of James II's invaders and thus initiated the siege of Derry in 1688.

One historian claims that the clan descended from Scottish kings and came to the Borders with Duncan.

A latter-day member of the family holds they came over with William the Conqueror, and indeed in Eskdale they were known as the De Irwyns. A Norman surname, however, was often adopted when clan to-names were out of favour.

An Irvine, it is said, sheltered Bruce when he was a fugitive and received lands in Drum, Aberdeenshire.

Their adventures in France when they, with other Scots, went with the Earl of Mar in 1407 to aid William of Bavaria, Count of Holland, are referred to in Wyntoun's Chronicle and also in an old French poem.

The Irvines were among the earliest clans in Eskdale. At one time they claimed all land between Esk and Nith. Their strong-hold was Stakeheuch (or Auchinrivock) on the very edge of the Debatable Land, where the Irvine Burn joins Esk, not far from Hollows.

The " List of Border Riders " drawn up by Musgrave, deputy Captain of Bewcastle about 1583, mentions the Urwens of Stake-heuch and their intermarriage with the Graems of Netherby. These intermarriages added to the confusion of the Border line, and Musgrave complains of the difficulty of bringing any of the culprits to justice because of the alliances on either side.

D

Curiously enough the best Irvine ballads are not " riding " ones but romantic. Fair Helen of Kirkconnel Lea is as well remembered as " Kinmont Willie." She was claimed as an Irving of Kirkconnel, a few miles over into Dumfriesshire. The rivals for her love are believed to have been Adam Fleming of Red Hill, and Bell of Blacket House. The ballad was quoted to me by a young officer in the First World War, who was descended from the Kirkconnel family: he said the tradition had been handed down from generation to generation. Helen favoured Fleming, and one day Bell lay in wait for them at their trysting place. Insane with jealousy, he pointed his musket at Fleming, but Helen flung herself on her lover's breast as he fired:

> I wish I were where Helen lies;
> Night and day on me she cries
> O that I were where Helen lies
> On fair Kirconnel Lea.
>
> Curst be the heart that thought the thought,
> And curst the hand that fired the shot,
> When in my arms burd Helen dropt
> And died to succour me.

Walking from Canonbie one day I climbed the steep knoll above the main road and found all that is left of Stakeheuch—a few stones built into a garden wall, with some " shot holes " still visible. The knoll falls sharply to the Irvine Burn on one side and the Esk in front. From the top of the tower it would be possible to see the warning bale-fire from Hollows.

Opposite Stakeheuch is Irvine House, which houses the offices of the Duke of Buccleuch's estates. The Tarras Water falls into the Esk opposite the house and the Irvine Burn flows through the grounds a little way to join the Esk, the Tarras Water and the Irvine Burn thus forming the boundary of the Debatable Land at this point.

Canonbie village follows the curve of the Esk enclosing Canonbie Lea and is sunny and sheltered. It is on the main road to Carlisle, which crosses the Border line about two miles further on. To follow this road, still through the old Debatable Land to the country of the Grahams, was my next objective.

Just outside the village, over the Esk on the " Hall Green," was the site of the Priory. It was pillaged by the English Army after the defeat of James V's army at Solway Moss. The usual decay would set in. Its stones would be handy for Canonbie bridge-builders, and, I strongly suspected, for the very substantial stone-built farm steadings close at hand. In the churchyard itself one genuine fragment of the ancient structure remains—a sedilia built into the tomb of a former minister.

The burn that passes down under the road and falls into the Esk is still called the Prior's Lynn. It is in the old names that one gets a clue to ancient locations, and the history of the land can be read. Celtic, Saxon, Norse, Norman, and even French names of the auld alliance, have all left records, both of nation-shaking events and small local happenings.

The country already began to have a decidedly English look, though this was still Scotland. Even the Esk had changed from its rocky course to a deep even flow through flat pastures. The fields were full of sleek cows.

" There's as guid kye in Cumberland," Buccleuch had remarked when Inglis offered him Branxholme in exchange for more in-land property, saying he was tired of having his stock raided by the Cumberland men.

The cow was all-important in those days. Crops were completely expendible. Stock could be driven within walls on a raid or moved about and hidden in hollows. A cow figures largely in all Border tales. There is the story of " Carey's Cow." Sir Richard Carey, the English Warden, was besieging the Scottish reivers who had taken refuge in Tarras Moss. A party slipped through and raided into England and carried off some of Carey's own stock. They sent him one of his own cows with their compliments " fearing lest he might fall short of provisions while in Scotland, they were sending him some English beef! "

And the Lauderdale cow that found its way home from the south. It had been in the train of one of the barons accompanying James VI to London. " How the deil did she get through the Borders? " asked James. " Where were the mosstroopers? "

Further on I came to Woodhouselee. The high scarp had every appearance of a tower site, and nearly always a " Woodhouse " was reminiscent of the first wooden " pele " that preceded the stone towers.

Would this be the bold Buccleuch's tower mentioned in " Kinmont Willie "? Tradition says the plot was first hatched at Woodhouselee and the details arranged at a race meeting in Langholm.

All that marked the transition between the two countries was two boards, " Cumberland," " Scotland," at the old Toll House. An old cottage just on the English side, however, had the Graham crest engraved above a lintel. I was into the English Grahams' country. Netherby was not far on. At this cottage a young man pointed out where the line of the " March Dyke," or Border line, came down from a wood above, crossed the road and continued on through fields to the Esk. He said part of the dyke itself could still be traced in the wood. When Logan Mack examined this part of the line some stretches of the dyke were well defined, but lumbering in the woods was beginning to spoil the best part of it. The dyke was really two parallel ditches with the excavated earth thrown up to form a mound, and it formed the Border line on land for some four miles between the rivers Sark and Esk. The estuary of the Solway and the River Sark formed the line up to the point where the dyke began.

I climbed to the wood to see how the 400-year-old dyke had fared. I don't think I could have traced it very far. The wood was dense with undergrowth: fallen branches and decayed leaves choked the ditches. Trees had fallen across, breaking the entrenchment. (And when, later, I followed the Border line from Gretna Green along Sark, I found the western end in an even worse state. The people at the farmhouse there, who remembered Logan Mack's visit nearly half a century before, led me through a tangle of bramble and brushwood to point out its disintegrated outline.) Nature was doing its best to wipe out an old score.

Back on the main road and over the Border line I was still in the Debatable Land. Taking the way over the level crossing at Scots Dyke station, down the lane and across a field I passed Kirkandrews Tower. It looked well preserved. It is a Netherby possession, but not the original " Netherby Ha' " of Scott's ballad " Lochinvar."

The church of Kirkandrews-on-Esk stands isolated in an old burial ground which contains some very ancient sculptured headstones. It is not attractive in appearance, but its setting is beautiful, on a wide bend of Esk. A notice in the porch gives an outline of its long and eventful history—typical of Border churches.

The parish was originally Scottish. In 1165 Turgot de Rossendale gave the church with everything pertaining to it to the Canons of Jedburgh.

Netherby Hall lies over the Esk and is reached by a footbridge, but it is in private grounds and I had been told Sir Fergus Graham was not at home. The Hall still has some relics of the original Ha', and the grounds comprise the site of the greatest northern civilian Roman camp. Those further north are military.

These Grahams of the Debatable Land were a perfect thorn in the flesh of the current English Warden. Their sympathies really lay with their Scots opposite numbers, for the English Grahams, it is said, were a branch that had left the Scottish Court after some quarrel with royalty. But they were ever ready to raid over the Border and were often engaged in some deadly feud with clans on the other side. A Graham is believed to have been in the garrison of Carlisle Castle and to have connived in the rescue of Kinmont Willie. "The Gallant Grahams," the ballads call them. The title goes back to the time of Wallace's great ally and friend, who fell at Falkirk.

The ballad of Hughie Grame in its several versions, as given in Child's *English and Scottish Ballads*, agrees that this freebooter was apprehended " for stealing of the Bishop's mare." Grame's wife was said to have been abducted by Bishop Aldridge of Carlisle, and Hughie made a retaliatory raid into Cumberland, carrying off the Bishop's favourite mare. Child thinks the tradition is taken from the ballad, the Bishop's name and the date being supplied from without. Allan Cunningham, whom he quotes, and Child himself, consider the mare simply qualifies as a fine one to mitigate the " ridiculousness " of making Hugh Grame steal a mare to retaliate for the wrong done him.

Ridiculousness! Not if I know my fellow Borderer! Compare Johnie Armstrong's equation of " a fat horse and a fair woman," the Laird's Jock's horse " worth gound and gude money," or indeed any of the horses that come into the mosstroopers' ballads.

Scott's version, he said, was procured from William Laidlaw of Blackhouse, with readings from Ritson's copy. The Lord Hume (Home) mentioned was warden of the East March, but the Homes had at one time possessions in Eskdale, in which was included Canonbie Priory.

Gude Lord Scroope's to the hunting gane,
  He has ridden ower moss and muir,
And he has grippit Hughie the Graeme
  For stealing o' the Bishop's mare. . . .

But as they were dealing their blows so free
  And baith sae bluidy at the time,
Ower the moss came ten yeomen sae tall
  A' for to tak brave Hughie the Graeme.

He is taken to Carlisle, tried and condemned.

Then up bespak him gude Lord Hume,
  As he sat by the judge's knee:
" Twenty white *ᵃ*owsen, my gude lord,   *ᵃ oxen*
  If you'll grant Hughie the Graeme to me."

The Bishop is adamant.

'Twas up and spak the gude Lady Hume,
  As she sat by the judge's knee:
" A peck of white pennies, my gude lord judge,
  If you'll grant Hughie the Graeme to me."

But the Bishop refuses her pleading. Hughie perceives his " auld
father " in court, " tearing his hair most piteously " :

" O haud your tongue, my father ", he says,
  " And see that ye dinna weep for me!
For they may ravish me o' my life
  But they canna banish me frae Heaven *ᵃ*hie."   *ᵃ high*

One is reminded of a later and greater Graham, Montrose, on
the scaffold of Edinburgh. The ballad ends:

" Here, Johnie Armstrang, tak thou my sword,
  That is made o' the metal sae fine,
And when thou comest to the English side,
  Remember the death of Hughie the Graeme."

Even after James VI came to the English throne it was said by
the English Commissioners " the people of Cumberland abhor and
fear the name of Graham . . . if the Grahams were not, the country

would soon be free of theft." The Royal Commission for the Settlement of the Borders in 1605 set about liquidating the Grahams as thoroughly as the Armstrongs. Their habitations were cleared out, if not destroyed; the Earl of Cumberland was " advised " that he should not even farm out his lands to wives or friends of the Grahams. Many were banished—150 from the Debatable Land were sent to serve in the garrisons of Flushing and Brill, and others to Ulster. But somehow they filtered back. In 1606 the English Commissioners wrote to the Earl of Salisbury:

> Many of the Grahams returned from the cautionary towns, some fugitives of that name and divers of those who broke out of Carlisle Castle, remained dispersed in Esk and the adjoining countries of Scotland with desire rather to hide themselves than to do much hurt. . . . We have committed to Carlisle Castle divers of the Grahams who have been neither offenders of late years, nor returned from cautionary towns. Their restraint will not a little bridle their friends who are out.

They also expressed the hope that " if a convenient number of men from both sides of the Border, inured from their youth upwards to blood and theft, were picked out or otherwise sent away, the rest would soon be reclaimed "; and they acted on that policy.

At Netherby the Esk is very broad and deep, and this stretch is particularly famous for its salmon. The salmon equalled the cow in importance, far back into the earliest monastic times. Here on the Border line it led to the last great clash between the English and Scottish Borderers. Right up to the settlement of the Border line there was trouble on the Esk. The English built " fish garths " which prevented the salmon from going up into Scottish waters, and as quickly as they were built the Scots demolished them.

In 1783 the old feud revived and what was known locally as the " battle of the coops " took place. The owner of Netherby had built a stone and wood barricade across the Esk where it passed through his land.

Such a clan rising had not been seen since " days of old." Armed with pitchforks, scythe blades, and muskets the Scots advanced on Netherby. On the English side was ranged a body of soldiers hastily summoned from Carlisle. A Scot started to break a hole in the garth. If the infantry fired the Scots would attack. But common sense prevailed, no shot was fired, and no blood shed.

The breach was made. But no Netherby owner ever again attempted to erect a fish garth.

As I turned from the Esk I met a shepherd and his two collies.

" Please could you tell me who lives in Kirkandrews Tower now ? " I asked.

" I do."

" Would your wife let me see over the tower ? "

" I am sure she would. Go on up and ask her."

I wondered how any wife would enjoy working in a centuries-old tower. I mounted stone steps to a door in the wall which in ancient times would have been reached by a ladder let down and drawn up again. No lady of the tower could have received me more graciously than the shepherd's wife. I was invited in. I stepped into the kitchen and got the surprise of my life. It was a de luxe model! Then I was shown two beautifully furnished bedrooms and a sitting-room, with their deepset " shot windows " framing entrancing views. After that I was quite prepared for the pale pastel-coloured bathroom. All this snugly within six-foot-thick walls!

It is a common saying in the Borders that a good shepherd is worth his weight in gold. This shepherd certainly lived like a prince.

I asked if I might climb to the top of the tower. Taking a powerful torch and handing me another, Mrs Bell opened a door on to a dark, twisting, narrow and worn stone stairway. The sudden transition was like stepping back into the fifteenth century. We came out on the bartizan where of old the lady of the tower would take the air, or the watching warriors keep a look-out for an approaching foe. Today all round lay the broad acres of Netherby. The Esk wound placidly into the pale afternoon sky.

I had walked the sole loose off one of my shoes and had forgotten to pack another pair. Mrs Waugh, of the Canonbie store, said there was no boot repairer, but I might try the cobbler.

" He only makes clogs for shepherds and farmers," she said. " He is the third of his generation in the trade. He might be able to fix you up."

" I can't walk in clogs," I said. " You have to learn to walk in them when you are young," said Mrs Waugh.

Feeling rather like a pony going to be shod I was led into the cobbler's workshop, which, with its open glowing fire, was really like a smithy. I was glad to see the old craftsman and his apprentice were still very busy. Here was one old craft that had not died out. He nailed down the loose sole but declined payment for " such a small job."

The Debatable Land had been practically cleared of reivers by the time of Charles I, but there remained one of the old breed of Armstrong, Christie's Will, who was said to have lived in Hollows Tower, and who gave rise to the diverting ballad in Scott's *Minstrelsy*. Child does not include it in his collection, and Scott admits that he has put it together from fragments current in the district. But it is a good story for all that, and entirely in keeping with the spirit of the Borderer.

I had not discovered any ballads relating to my grandmother's own clan—the Moffats (originally De Monteult)—in Eskdale. Bruce gave them charters to lands in Westerkirk for their support at Bannockburn. There were Moffats in the Knock in 1504, and they were still in possession in 1607, and remained as tenants of the Duke of Buccleuch until 1905.

Nor had I found anyone who could prove descent from Johnie Armstrong. But before I finally left Canonbie a Miss Maimie Armstrong (who did not claim descent, but whose family had farmed their land for three hundred years till the male line failed) said to me:

" There was an old pedlar, William Armstrong, who lived in Cauldside, Canonbie. He claimed to be the direct descendant of Johnie Armstrong, and had the family tree. He died many years ago and it passed to his relatives in Hawick, but whether of the same name I do not know."

IV

" Many a Crest that is Famous in Story "

I N Liddesdale and the Debatable Land Scott had found some of his best ballads: in Eskdalemuir he found the germ of his own first long poem in the story of " Gilpin Horner." The lovely young Countess of Dalkeith had, Scott tells us, " enjoined on me as a task to compose a ballad on the subject." The result was *The Lay of the Last Minstrel*, which brought him fame.

It was to find the site of the legend of Gilpin Horner that I now turned aside into Eskdalemuir. It is one of the most sequestered dales in the south of Scotland. There is not even an inn in its entire length between Langholm and Tushielaw in Ettrick. Yet it is easily entered by several roads. I have travelled them all, except that from Lockerbie, and found them all equally attractive. It is also a through route from the Border line to Edinburgh, through some of the most enchanting country in the Borders, ballad-sung and legend-haunted.

The road from Langholm branches at Enzieholm Bridge. That to the left leads to the Black Esk and continues by the fort of Castle O'er down into Eskdalemuir village: that on the right crosses the White Esk and passes the prehistoric stone circles known locally as the " Girdle Stanes " and the " Lowpin' Stanes " to Hartmanor and the Roman camp at Raeburnfoot. Here it re-crosses the White Esk and joins up with the other road, and a single road now goes on to Ettrick Valley. Both of these branch roads keep the Esk in sight and pass through sections of the Castle O'er Forest.

But there is another road from the Ewes Valley at Ewes Kirk and the site (marked by a tablet) of the birthplace of Henry Scott Riddell, shepherd-poet and later minister of Teviothead. This is the road with the alluring title " The Gates of Eden," which, it is pleasant to note, was bestowed on it by a divine of the City Temple, London. Narrow, twisting, and climbing through a gap of the hills it seems given over entirely to the wandering sheep. At Burnfoot, down in Eskdalemuir, it crosses the Esk and joins the main road short of Enzieholm.

I arrived at Hartmanor on the heels of departing archaeologists. They had been excavating at Raeburnfoot under the leadership of Miss Annie Robertson of the Hunterian Museum, Glasgow. This valley, with its Roman camp, and prehistoric settlements and forts on almost every hill, could be a rich field for archaeologists. It is in the very heart of Strathclyde, the old British kingdom. The Esk is said to be a Cymric name. Mystical, elusive, the Celtic influence lingered on in song and legend. Their pagan rites are still commemorated, in all innocence, in rural customs.

I was on a different quest from that of the archaeologists, yet our aims and ends were the same—to gain knowledge and understanding of the past. What they sought in stone and shard I sought in song and story. We shared the same enthusiasms, the same delight in discovery. And when we go back to our desks the memories of our hours of field work, hours spent in the open air, of the scent of heath and peat, and the ever-changing colours of the hills, will remain.

The first day I set out to walk by Watcarrick to Enzieholm Bridge, some seven miles, where I expected to pick up the school bus returning from Langholm Academy about four o'clock.

I crossed the bridge at Raeburnfoot to the village, and turned left. Past the eighteenth-century manse I came to an old graveyard and the site of the Chapel of Watcarrick referred to in 1592 and which served Upper Eskdalemuir until the Reformation. The graveyard is full of ancient tombstones of the Beatisons, who were the dominant clan here after the Douglases—against whom they fought. They were notorious reivers, came under English " assurance " after severe raids by Lord Wharton, and eventually were numbered among the broken men.

How they lost their lands—all but " Wudcarrick "—to the Scotts, was told with other traditions to Sir Walter Scott by Mr Beattie, the Laird of Meikledale of that day, and used by Scott for his *Lay*. Scott maintains that in his day " the old people give locality to the story by showing the ' Gaillard's Haugh,' the place where Buccleuch's men were concealed." It may not be history, but it is at least glorious fiction.

Here too is where Gilpin Horner, the elf, was reputed to appear at milking time, frightening but never harming the milkmaids. In the latter half of the seventeenth century, among witnesses cited in an enquiry was a Thomas Bell who declared it had " flesh and blood like other folk."

The elf was probably some unfortunate dwarf.

Groups of rhododendrons, shrubs, and specimen trees began to appear among the native trees and seemed to mark where a house and " pleasaunce " had once been. This would be the home of Richard Bell, the naturalist, where he wrote his book, *My Strange Pets*. His father had changed the original name of Yetbyre to Castle O'er after the large British fort on the hill opposite. This did not please Richard Bell, who believed the old name signified " Chief's Stronghold."

It might well have applied to a stronghold of a Bell in the reiving days. The great leader of the Border branch of the Bells was William Bell of Blacket House, " Red Cloak," a tenant of Douglas of Drumlanrig. He married an Agnes Grahame, which did not, however, prevent him taking " 150 kine and oxen and 60 sheep and spoiling the house of Grahame to the extent of £700 " and continuing a deadly feud with the English Grahames. In 1606 he was prohibited from " hunting in Cheviot or destroying the woods." He closed his adventurous career by being nominated " to assist in the pacification of the Borders."

For adherence to the cause of Charles I Blacket House was burned; while George Bell of Scotsburgh and Godsburgh was fined £1,000 for adhering to the Covenant.

Benjamin Bell of Blacket House (born 1794) was the eminent surgeon. He sold Blacket House and other estates to educate himself and the younger members of his family. Among his descendants was another well-known surgeon, Joseph Bell (1837–1911), said to have been the original of Sherlock Holmes.

About here the Castle O'er Forest begins. The dark, somewhat sombre, lines of the conifers were lightened at the roadside by hardwood trees. The Forestry Commission is doing splendid work in reclaiming wastelands, but I would like to see more planting of hardwood deciduous trees to mark the changing seasons. I miss, too, the clean lines of the bare hills and the companionship of sheep.

When the forest ends and the road descends to the junction of the Black with the White Esk (the " black " runs over peat and moss; the " white " is crystal clear over sand and pebble) I came on two intriguing place names: " King Shaw's Grave," and " Handfasting Haugh." The grave was a tumulus which stood in the Airdshaw Moss. Like all these prehistoric stones, whose origin had long been lost, it had acquired a name and tradition in local lore. Here, it was said, a great battle took place between the Picts and Scots. The Scots were victors, and the Pictish King Shaw was drowned in the deep pool where the two Esks meet, still called the King's Pool. This pool, however, has another local interpretation of the name—the haunt of a fabulous " king " fish.

Down here in the glen where the forest, with its neat orderly man-planted trees, receded, the Black Esk was like a dark and mysterious runnel eddying out of primitive hills, as if it had never known human comings and goings. Yet on the flattish haugh above the White Esk there was once a flourishing township where a big annual fair was held. There the ancient marriage custom of " handfasting " would often be performed. With hands clasped the couple would bind themselves to live together as man and wife for one year. If the arrangement worked well they would return to have their bond ratified by a " book-o-bosom " priest. These priests were so called because they travelled the countryside carrying a book of the Gospels in their gowns. If the couple wished to separate, any offspring of the union were legitimised.

From the creeks of Galloway over the hills and down the Black Esk the smugglers brought their goods into Eskdalemuir.

From here to Enzieholm Bridge the valley became gradually homely with farmhouses and cottages, rich river pastures, and light woodlands and tree-lined lanes.

As at Trimontium in Melrose, excavation at Raeburnfoot had only been permitted on the understanding that it was all to be filled in again and the land returned to farming. Now, having travelled so long in this once ravaged Border land I hardly blame the farmers. Every now and then the plough or the bulldozer will turn up some archaeological treasure. Only recently a prehistoric cist with burial vessels was unearthed near Lockerbie.

Raeburn was the " Moodlaw " of the Raeburn Scotts, from whom Sir Walter Scott traced his descent.

The grave of Andrew Hislop the Covenanter is on the hillside above Craighaugh. He was shot on the spot by Claverhouse at the insistence of Sir James Johnstone of Westerhall, on 12 May 1685. I found the weathered inscription difficult to decipher, but the commission on Ancient Monuments, which prints it, says it is of eighteenth-century character and had been recut.

Hislop was a young lad, one of the many who had to take to the hills. Claverhouse searched his mother's cottage and then traced him to the hillside. It is said that Claverhouse had not wanted to shoot, but Johnstone, who was an implacable opponent of the Covenanters, insisted. The lad refused to be blindfolded and died praising God. Claverhouse lodged in Langholm the night after the shooting, and his landlady told afterwards of his restless pacing up and down in his room. " Bloody Clavers," or " Bonnie Dundee "—depending on whichever side you were on; but he was a " gallant Graham," and, as an opponent said, " Every inch a gentleman."

There were more Covenanters than Cavaliers in the Scottish Borders, more Presbyterians than Episcopalians and Catholics. The Covenanters were fighting their own War of Independence. " Indeed the country had not been so moved since the days of Wallace and Bruce," as Trevelyan says. Once more the Border hills were full of hunted men. They were like the old mosstroopers, hiding by day, and by night going to their open-air conventicles by devious ways: " on solitary hillsides, in the scoop of the burn, or the heart of the birch wood, with sentinels set all round to watch for the approach of the red dragoons." And they sang—how they sang! Bishop Leslie had written of the singing mosstroopers, but now it was the psalms that echoed in these lonely hillsides.

Craighaugh-Johnstone, the lovely home of Sir Gordon and Lady Lethem, is just below the hillside, on old Johnstone lands. The White Esk skirts their garden, the hills slope down gently on either side. Directly across the road is a hill fort and, within sight, the Roman camp.

The Roman road passed through Craighaugh and went up by Raeburnfoot to Craik Cross, a signal post. There is a magnificent view there on a clear day—to the Solway and beyond, and all the familiar Border landmarks can be seen. Then it goes down to Howpasley, one of the remotest villages in Teviotdale and where the Thirlestane Scotts originated.

Ettrick Pen, from which the Esk rises, closes the upper end of the valley. It is seen much better from this side than from Ettrick. It can be climbed by way of Glendearg, " the red glen," where the last wolf is said to have been shot.

The road, after crossing Esk by an old and narrow stone bridge, the nearest to its source, rises to a summit of about 1,000 feet.

Davington on the hillside was an early possession of the How-pasley Scotts and later a refuge for a deposed Thirlestane branch. In the Borders the ballad of " The Dowie Howms of Yarrow " is said to be based on the killing of a Scott of Thirlestane by a Scott of Tushielaw. Young Thirlestane was a younger brother of Sir Robert Scott of Thirlestane, and he left a son who later became laird by transfer from John Scott, the real heir, who is said to have jeopardised his life and lost his means through his loyalty to the King under Montrose. John Scott retired to Davington and that line became farmers round about Moffat. Lord Napier had a curious story to tell, though the woman could produce no proof:

A few years ago I met a beggar on the road near Thirlestane, and she told me she had a large family, and that her forbears had been lairds of all the country round about . . . the name was Scott, and a descendant of Davington.

Craig-Brown, who quotes the story (*History of Selkirkshire*), adds:

a relation of this woman, William Scott, served in the 90th Regiment from 1794–1817 under Major General Mark Napier, a Scott of Thirlestane, who thus unconsciously commanded his chief for twenty three years!

One can see how Sir Walter Scott, digging diligently into family history, got plenty of material for his romances.

Dumfedling, further on, had a long history as a barony of feudal times, with a justice court. Foulbog, down in a deep glen, and Bloodhopeburn—sinister names—is the region of reputed buried treasure. As an old rhyme says:

> Between the wet ground and the dry
> The gold of Eskdalemuir doth lie.

There was enough gold on the Eskdalemuir hills that sunny autumn when I revisited them, in the bracken and bent. I have never seen so much bent elsewhere except in Tweedsmuir.   There is no heather at all.

The road descends again and the valley of the Esk drops out of sight and the crowding names of all the great feudal houses of Douglas, Lindsay, Avenel, Lovel, and Maxwell; and the clans of Moffat, Johnstone, Bell and Beatison, that have in turn held sway, sound as but faint echoes on the empty hillsides.

The road crosses the Selkirkshire boundary and is now in the country of the Scotts, held from " time immemorial " to the present day.   Wherever the ballads are sung, wherever the reiving days are recalled, the Thirlestane Scotts are known.   They had a position in the Borders second only to Buccleuch, and one writer on heraldry says:

> While a male heir of Thirlestane was alive neither Harden, placed by Burke as chieftain, nor any other branch of Scott could succeed to the chieftainship of the Scotts.

Be that as it may, the Thirlestane Scotts can trace their descent directly from a John Scott of Howpasley who was Laird of Thirlestane in 1536.   Earlier origins are obscure and consequently controversial.   Satchells claims their descent from Buccleuch but there seems no family tree to prove it.

The old knight Sir Robert Scott of Thirlestane-in-Ettrick was as renowned as " Auld Maitland " of Thirlestane-in-Lauder. Satchells says Buccleuch consulted him first before embarking on the rescue of Kinmont Willie.   Thirlestane immediately offered him 500 men.   But the " bold Buccleuch "

> Thanked him for their vote and said that must not be.
> " Pick me out chosen men not more than thirty three."

William and Walter Scott of Thirlestane as younger sons went to the raid.

I suppose that up to that extraordinary union of a warlike Border clan and a family of scientists and intellectuals the history of Thirlestane Tower was that of many another Border pele of note.   But since a Scott of Thirlestane married, in 1669, the Mistress of Napier and brought that notable peerage into the family, to the shades of their ancestors are now added " wizards," cava-

PLATE 2
Harden Glen
House

Photograph:
Scotsman
Publications Ltd.

PLATE 3
Hermitage
Castle

*Photograph:
G. Douglas
Bolton*

liers, generals, admirals, ambassadors, governors, and men of letters.

One of the most fascinating family histories I have read is that compiled by Francis, twelfth Lord Napier. Reading, I walked the streets of old Edinburgh with these distinguished Napiers— Provosts, Ambassadors to England, Denmark, and Burgundy. And while the fascinating and disturbing Mary, Queen of Scots, was upsetting not only the capital but the whole kingdom, the first " wizard " appears. Of him the Queen's Secretary, Claude Nun, is writing:

> The laird of Markyston [Merchiston] who had the reputation of being a great wizard, made lots with several persons to the amount of 500 crowns, that by 5th May Her Majesty would be out of Loch Leven Castle.

She escaped 2 May 1568. Perhaps Napier had inside knowledge?

And at Merchiston, his son, who is to become the real wizard, the inventor of logarithms, is born in 1550, and in the same year as he is born the first Laird of Thirlestane, John Scott, dies. The " Inventor " writes " A Plain Discovery of the Revelation of St John " and invents a cannon. Its efficiency and potential powers of destruction appal him and he buries it and all its construction plans. His Merchiston tenants consider he is a warlock, and his pet black fowl his familiar spirit. He marries twice and by his second wife has ten children. One of them is the last " wizard " of the house. He, too, is a celebrated mathematician, but he writes a book on Alchemy. This scares him with its potentialities for evil even more than the cannon did his father, and in a dedication he adjures his " posterity " by most solemn and sacred oaths " not to make it public, nor to communicate it to any living soul, unless it be a child of the arts, a good man fearing God, and who will cherish the secret of Hermes." He is still in the age of mingled piety and superstition. . . .

Seventy lances Thirlestane had brought to the service of James V, when the other nobles had refused to follow him in a war against England, and in recognition the family received the charter of arms with its fleur-de-lis, similar to the tressure in the royal arms, a bundle of spears, and the motto " Ready, aye ready."

The Scotts' old loyalty to the monarchy continued through the

E

Napiers. They fought for Charles I and II, and the fortunes of their house suffered with them. At Philiphaugh Lord Napier and his son were of that gallant band who rallied round Montrose, fought their way through the enemy ranks and escaped up Yarrow.

I had hoped to see some of the Montrose relics in Thirlestane House, but I was told they had been removed, and that some were in America. The mystery of what became of Montrose's heart has never been solved. It is said Montrose promised his heart to Lady Napier, and that when his trunk was thrown into a pit in the Boroughmuir after his execution, she had the grave secretly opened and the heart brought to her. Encased in a silver casket it had the most extraordinary wanderings until it was finally lost.

The beautiful Sarah Lennox, the only woman George III wanted to marry, married a younger son of the seventh Lord Napier and had three very distinguished sons, all generals, including the conqueror of Scinde who sent the famous telegram: " Peccavi."

Perhaps the most modern note to be recorded about the Napiers is that the Russians, having photographed the hidden side of the moon and named its salient features after eminent scientists, thus honoured John Napier.

Below Thirlestane House there is a 700-year-old mill-lade at Gamescleuch. The name Thirlestane signifies a millstone to which the tenants of certain farms were " thirled," or bound, to send their grain to be ground. A contemporary document refers to a dispute over the possession of Gamescleuch between a Scott of Thirlestane and a Scott of Tushielaw, which may have led to the theory that this was the cause of the duel and the origin of " The Dowie Howms of Yarrow," though that ballad under the title of " The Braes of Yarrow " has many versions, in which the relationships differ. But the ballads often took a universal theme and related them to local events, without particularising exact relationships. And as I have remarked earlier, the Scandinavian influence appears in many Border ballads. Hogg's version, communicated to Scott, is the one popularly accepted in the Borders.

And now after this detour, I must return to Langholm, by way of Burnfoot in Eskdalemuir, and Wauchope.

Burnfoot, which lies at the foot of the " Gates of Eden " is the last living link with the Douglases in Eskdale. The owner is a younger son of the late Palmer Douglas of Cavers and inherited it from his grandmother, a Malcolm. He can therefore claim descent from both the hero of Otterburn and the Malcolms of Burnfoot, who have a semi-legendary descent from the ancient Celtic kings of Scotland.

The first mention of the Douglases in Eskdale is in 1319, when they received lands from Bruce, with whom they had fought at Bannockburn. But Sir William, the father of " good Sir James," and Sir Alexander Lindsay of Wauchope, had also fought earlier with Wallace; and later James, Earl of Douglas, and Alexander Lyndsay fought together at Otterburn.

It was at Staplegorton in Eskdalemuir in the reign of David I that the charter to the lands in Annandale was given to the great-grandfather of Bruce, and Bruce confirmed the Eskdale lands to the Douglases by the famous " Emerald Charter." An emerald ring was placed on the finger of good Sir James by Bruce himself to confirm the bond. What became of the ring is one of the unsolved mysteries of history. Was it still on the hand of Douglas when he was killed in the fight with the infidel on the way to the Holy Land, and looted from his dead body?

> Good Sir James Douglas
>   Who wight, wise and worthy was
> Was ne'er overglad for no wyning
>   Nor yet o'er sad for no ᵃtyning   ᵃ *losing*
> Good fortune and evil chance
>   He weighed both in the balance.

Elevated by Robert II to a position only a little lower than the throne, the Douglas family became too powerful for the subsequent Stuart kings. It was James II who finally broke their power, taking the advice of Cardinal Beaton to " divide and conquer." He set the " Red " Douglas (Angus) against the " Black." As Hume of Godscroft put it:

> The last battell the Earl of Douglas was at the Earl of Angus discomfited him; so that it became a proverb: " The Red Douglas put down the black "—those of the House of Angus being of the fairer complexion.

That " last battell " was at Arkinholm: the Scotts, Johnstones, Maxwells, Beatisons, Carlyles, and Glendennings were all united against the Black Douglas.

The first Malcolm came from Lochore in Fife, a Robert Malcolm, M.A., who was " presented " to Ewes Kirk 1717 by the Earl of Dalkeith. The stipend was so small that the Earl gave him also the farm of Burnfoot at a nominal rent. One son, George, managed the farm and married Margaret Pasley of the neighbouring estate. Four of their sons became knights, " the four knights of Eskdale "; James, John, Pulteney and Charles. Sir John's monuments are on Whita Hill and in Westminster Abbey: soldier, Governor of Bombay, and historian, his *Life of Clive* is said to have inspired Macaulay's *Essay on Clive*, and one of his Persian legends Matthew Arnold's *Sohrab and Rustum*. Sir Pulteney's statues stand in Langholm and in St Paul's: Admiral, the naval commander at St Helena, he won the regard and admiration of the imprisoned Napoleon.

Like William and Dorothy Wordsworth who, in passing through Langholm, do not seem to have " turned aside " to visit Wauchope, I, too, had hitherto omitted this loveliest of secluded little glens. Wordsworth, who visited it on a later day, was moved to write a sonnet.

Wauchope is mentioned in 1281 as the domain of the Lindsays: it is also the site of the ballad of " Archie o' Cawfield," which is in all essentials a repetition of " Jock o' the Side." The Roman road passes Calfield over into Eskdalemuir.

The Lindsays do not seem to have had a long connexion with Eskdale, and there is some confusion among historians as to where the Wauchope Lindsays' loyalty lay—with England or Scotland. Their castle here at Wauchope, of which nothing now remains, must have been strongly defensive, perched on a plateau over thirty feet above the Wauchope Water in a triangle formed by the junction of the Becks burn with the Wauchope, and on the north east and south east sides there seems to have been an artificial fosse. In Dacre's raid after Flodden he boasted he had laid waste almost the whole of Ewesdale and Eskdale.

No man dwelleth in them after this day, save only the touns of Annan, Stepel [Staplegorton], Wauchope.

One might wonder how, after such raids, the people were not completely exterminated. But in this country of huddled hills, deep gullies, and morasses, there were abundant hiding-places. There was a well-established system of warnings by bale-fires and other means. The people could take to the hills with what stock they could drive, and return when the invaders had passed. Their dwellings were mere hovels of turf and wood, easily laid waste but as soon rebuilt. When the stone towers succeeded the wooden peles they were more often evacuated than defended. They could be fired, but not until the advent of cannon could the walls be destroyed.

Lindsay's castle was probably built in the late thirteenth century after Sir John Lindsay had received his charter from Alexander III; and the Lindsays held it, with a short forfeiture, till 1505. Maxwell, as Warden, had a brief tenure of land there in return for " stanching of thift and other misreule."

St Bride's Chapel—the earliest church in Eskdale—has also completely disappeared, only the " Chapel Stone " marking its supposed site. Wauchope Kirk (1606) was attached to Canonbie. Here we meet the Armstrongs again—in 1610 in company with Irvings, Littles and Grahams and " thirteen other surnames " refusing to pay their teinds—" Lambistiend, Stirkestiend, and uther tiend, chees and hay tiend," and " put to the horn " for failing to appear on summons.

Built into the wall of the kirkyard I noticed some fine carved stones. An incised sword, believed to be of thirteenth-century English design, may have belonged to an English Lindsay.

V

Wild Liddesdale

NOVEMBER HAD SET IN before I was back on the Border line
again. It was to be a quick " foray " from Melrose. The
suggestion was Bobbie's. He is a bus driver, but has his
own little car and he was on holiday. A Borderer born and bred,
he is as keen as a hound on any Border trail.

Beginning where I had left off at Underburnmouth, we turned
right down a short road to Kershopefoot. This is where the Border
line leaves the Liddel and travels for nine miles or so up the Kershopeburn to Lamisik ford, where it takes to the hills, sometimes following
small burns, or crossing bogs and climbing over ridges, taking in
the new Kershope Forest which begins at Kershopefoot. This
part of the line to Carter Bar is only for those who wish to do it the
hard way! But the first part, up the forest road by the side of the
burn, is easy and a delightful walk.

The railway line crosses the Kershopeburn where it enters the
Liddel a little to the east of the station, and I suppose few pass-
engers in the express trains notice the boards on either side, " Scotland," " England," or are aware they have crossed the Border.

This is perhaps the most famous spot in all reiving ballads, for it
was here that Willie Armstrong, " Kinmont Willie," was captured
on a " day of truce." The English might say he was on the wrong
side of the water, but they could not get away from the fact that
the time of truce had not expired: " All persones whatsoever that
came to these meetings sould be saife fra' the tyme of the meetings
of the Wardaines or their deputies till the nixt day of the sun
rysing." Such was the Border law. At these Wardens' Meetings
all business between the two kingdoms was conducted; complaints
were heard and justice administered. A great deal of it, of course,
dealt with claims for compensation for raids.

" Kinmont Willie " was a well-known reiver the English
Wardens had long sought but had failed to implicate. On his way

[58]

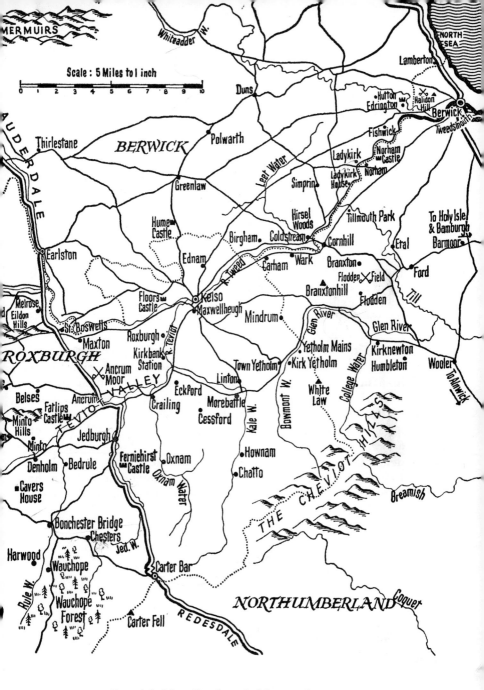

Berwickshire, Roxburghshire, and
County of Northumberland.

home from the Wardens' Meeting at Kershopefoot by way of the Liddel he was ambushed and taken to Carlisle. Lord Scrope was at that time English Warden under Elizabeth and Buccleuch Warden under James VI, but it was their deputies who were at the Kershope meeting—Salkeld and Robert Scott.

The place of this meeting, by the Liddel, is still called " Turner-holm," a corruption of Tourneyholm perhaps, for in the earlier days disputes were settled by single combat. Local tradition named a standing stone there " The Laird's Jock's Stone."

Kinmont Willie's capture posed a delicate problem for Buccleuch. Personally, he was outraged but he did not wish to embroil James VI who, as the hopeful heir of Elizabeth, was going warily. His repeated demands for redress and release of the prisoner were ignored and in the end he took matters into his own hands. When the news of the rescue of Kinmont Willie from Carlisle Castle reached Queen Elizabeth she " stormed not a little," wrote a sharp letter to her Warden and demanded the surrender of Buccleuch. James VI, to his credit, stood up to Elizabeth in defence of his Warden, but eventually Buccleuch delivered himself up.

The ballad takes the usual liberties to glorify the clan involved—in this instance the Scotts, though there were, according to Scrope's list, several Armstrongs, including the Laird of Mangerton, a son of Gilnockie and four sons of Kinmont. Poetical justice also demanded the death of the " fause Sakelde," though actually no English were killed. The only known version of the ballad is that in Scott's *Minstrelsy*, and is one of the most popular of the Border ballads.

> O have ye na heard o the fause Sakelde?
> O ha' ye na heard o the keen Lord Scroop?
> How they hae ta'en ᵃbauld Kinmont Willie,   *ᵃ bold*
> On Hairibee to hang him up?

Manacled, Willie is taken to Carlisle Castle and delivered to Lord Scrope, whom he defies:

> " My hands are tied, but my tongue is free,
> And whae will daur this deed avou?
> Or answer by the Border law?
> Or answer to the bauld Buccleu'? "

" Now haud thy tongue, thou rank reiver!
There's never a Scot shall set thee free;
Before ye cross my castle-gate,
I trow ye shall take farewell o' me."

" Fear na ye that, my lord," quo' Willie;
By the faith o' my body, Lord Scroop," he
said,
" I never yet lodged in a hostelrie
But I paid my ^{*a*}lawing before I gaed."   *^a reckoning*

When Buccleuch gets word his wrath is terrible. He strikes the
table and " gaurd the red wine spring on hie ":

" O were there war between the lands,
As well I wat that there is nane,
I would slicht Carlisle Castell high,
Tho' it were builded of marble-stane . . .

" But since nae war's between the lands,
And there is peace, and peace should be,
I'll neither harm English lad or lass
And yet the Kinmont freed shall be! "

How the Buccleuch kept his word makes exciting reading:

And as we cross'd the Batable Land,
When to the English side we held,
The first o' men that we met wi',
Whae suld it be but fause Sakelde!

The Scots borderer is willing to halt in any enterprise and engage
in argument or repartee, and this they do with Salkeld, as told in
the next five stanzas.
But Dickie o' Dryhope (an Armstrong) having no " lear "
(learning) cuts it short by thrusting his lance " thro' his fause
bodie."
They reach the swollen Eden, but get across. The April night
develops into a storm of " wind and weet and fire and sleet."
They leave their horses lest they makes a noise and creep up to the
Castle walls. The watchman is overpowered.

" Nou sound out, trumpets! " quo' Buccleuch;
" Let's wauken Lord Scroop richt merrilie! "
Then loud the Warden's trumpets blew
" O wha daur meddle wi' me? " . . .

They thocht King James and a' his men
    Had won the house wi' bow and spear;
It was but twenty Scots and ten
    That put a thousand in ᵃsic a ᵇsteer!   ᵃ *such* ᵇ *stir*

They reach the inner prison, and the rescue is effected in much the same manner as in "Jock o' the Side"; and as Kinmont Willie is carried down on the shoulders of Red Rowan he calls out:

" Fareweil, fareweil, my gude Lord Scroop!
    My gude Lord Scroop, fareweil! " he cried;
" I'll pay you for my lodging-mail,
    When first we meet on the border-side."

Carlisle bells ring out to muster horse and foot, and led now by Lord Scrope, they follow in hot pursuit:

Buccleuch has turned to Eden Water,
    Even where it flow'd from bank to brim,
And he has plunged in wi' a' his band,
    And safely swam them thro' the stream.

He turned him to the other side,
    And at Lord Scroop his gluve flung he;
" If ye like na my visit ᵃin merry England,   ᵃ *into*
    In fair Scotland come visit me! "

All sore astonished stood Lord Scroop
    He stood as still as rock of stane.
He scarcely dared to ᵃtrew his eyes   ᵃ *believe*
    When thro' the water they had gane.

" He is either himsel a devil from hell,
    Or else his mother a witch ᵃmaun be;   ᵃ *must*
I wad na have ridden that wan water
    For a' the ᵇgowd in Christentie."   ᵇ *gold*

Keeping to the English Cumberland side of the burn we followed the uphill road from the station to a bridge. From here, straight up the burn, through what is now Kershope Forest, was the old raiding road between Liddesdale and North Tynedale.

We turned right on the road to Longtown by Penton, and we had not gone far when we saw a tall grey house standing gauntly above the road. This was Stanegarthside, " the Captain of Bewcastle's house " in the ballad of " Jamie Telfer of the Fair Dodhead."

There was a tower at Dodhead in Ettrick, where Scott places his version of the ballad, but there is a Dodburn in Teviotdale, also claimed as the site. Ettrick tradition claims the Scotts are the heroes of the fray: in Teviotdale it is claimed for the Elliots. Scott thinks it probable that both clans took part and each claimed the honour of the day. He gives the only known version.

In this ballad the theme is the rescue of Jamie Telfer's stolen kye, and the whole ballad is a vivid description of a typical Border raid, with a map of the countryside, and a roll call of the clans.

The topography also gives a good idea of the extent of the Buccleuch overlordship. Today tenancies have changed, but the farms remain, and there is no better way of becoming familiar with the countryside than by following the place-names of the old ballads.

This ballad, it has been surmised, must have been written by an eye-witness who was also something of a poet: " the gryming of a new-fa'n snaw "; " the bickering hail "; " the lyart locks o' Harden's hair." Scott is silent as to where he got his version. Was The Flower of Yarrow's adopted son the originator? But that story belongs to Harden.

This was the last of the " riding ballads " I was to encounter until I came to the Reidswire on Carter Bar. As one by one I had re-read these ballads and related them to their localities I had experienced a growing respect for the mosstroopers. It is not a question of " romanticising " them. As a race they had never become degraded, never degenerated into mere ruffians or bandits. They had their base members and these they despised. They were men of undisciplined emotions, they " grat " as easily as they laughed, and they were ready to risk everything to rescue a " billy " or even a " billy's kye." If they were brutal, it was a brutal age. The menace of their times removed, they settled down to become the best agriculturalists in Scotland, and those Border clans which had been always foremost in the fray were to supply some of Scotland's most famous sons. The metamorphosis of the moss-troopers is a fascinating study.

The day was yet young and we decided to go on and find Liddel Mote and the meeting of the waters of Liddel and Esk.

The road from Stanegarthside runs high and gives a fine view of the Liddel valley. Musgrave wrote to Burleigh in 1583:

> I understand your lordship is not well acquainted with the names of the waters and dwelling places of the Riders and Evil doers both of Scotland and England,

and then proceeds to list them:

> The river Lydal is a fayre ryver, and hath her course down Liddesdale, so has the dale the name of the ryver. The ryver is all Scottische until it come to Kersoppffoote, planted with Ellotes, until it come neure Wheatoughe towre, then Armestronges inhabit it on both sydes, until it come to Kyrsoppffoote where it takes the dyvision of the realmes from Kyrsopp: then the Armstronges have the one syde and the English Fosters the other syde . . . so it [Liddel] runneth into the ryver called Eske.

This stretch of the Border line from Kyrsopp, or Crysopp (Kershope) along the Liddel and Esk to the foot of Leven Water was so notorious that a special watch had to be set nightly. The watch was also provided with bloodhounds to track down any marauders who got over the line.

Liddel Mote, or Moat, was in the country of the Graemes, but it has a history that stretches back long before their day even into mythical times. It was a British fort, which the Romans would make use of while at Netherby. The Roman road skirts its base. Then it became the medieval " Foss de Liddell." But there is a good deal of confusion in old records between Liddel Mote and Liddel Castle, which is nearer to Hermitage.

In 1319 Edward II was having trouble because " the best and richest of the country about Gillesland and Lydell [had] gone over to the enemy, except people of no account, more than 97 from the barony of Lydell alone." An interesting commentary on the relationship on either side of the Border line.

We found the Mote at last at the end of a " No thoroughfare " road to the farms of Little and Lower Moat. The Mote itself was difficult to trace. A plantation covers most of it and the railway embankment cuts through it. Beyond the railway we could see where the waters of Liddel and Esk meet at the beautiful Willow Pool.

In this region, tradition says, was fought the great battle of

Ardderyd in 573 from which the legendary Merlin fled, as told in the Welsh triads:

> The battle of Arterid, between the sons of Elifer and Gwendoleu, the son of Keidiau, and in this battle Gwendoleu fell. Merlin became insane.

The battle is stated to have lasted for forty-nine days, and left 40,000 slain. The Border tradition is that Merlin fled, a haunted man, to wander in the wilds of Tweedsmuir until he was stoned to death and cast into Tweed by shepherds who ignorantly feared him.

Merlin had prophesied victory for Gwendoleu—all the portents had been favourable—and he was to see Gwendoleu slain and all the gold torques of the great chiefs laid in the dust.

These Cymric bards were the earliest Border minstrels. Some of the medieval ballads were taken from the Arthurian cycle. Their spell still hangs over the land. I was reminded of a young American ex-serviceman, Carver Collins, who had served in the Second World War, and on sailing down the Forth homeward bound, had promised himself a return to Scotland. Eleven years later the promise was fulfilled, and I would like to quote a few lines of the fine poem he wrote inspired by the story of Merlin:

> ... and we who fought calamitously
> for only our right to read from the book of nature ...
> what was exceptional in what we did? ...
> No sailor ever wet his oar in salt surf
> that could not plot from flowing skies
> the compass of his course;
> no dresser of plain turf
> would put one foot in his furrow
> until his weather eye had been west.
> Yet when I did no more threatening a deed
> there were followers of yours
> ready to heap stones upon me where I stood. ...
> They were rich torques of beaten sunbeam
> we wore looped upon our necks. ...
> they were kind days of courtliness,
> they were nights deep with study,
> and the sharp excursions made by the valorous
> over the sword-sweep of our borders
> were to keep them so. ...

It was sorely done, though,
   to come down from the hill,
down from the hill was where we faltered
   and broke upon a wave of charge
that should have broke on us.
   For the days of your battle remember,
keep the heights about you,
   keep the heights. . . .

But I am old, Gwendydd, I am old,
   and shepherds have their dogs on me,
not that I play the wolf with them
   but that I might. . . .

There should be peace. . . .
   the land possesses riches too plenteous
for the histories of both our peoples to exhaust. . . .
   There should be peace. . . .

Penton Bridge, over the beautifully wooded Liddel linns, caused a detour. Here the Liddel, which had looked so mild and clear further up, is " drumly and dark." The centre of the bridge is the Border line. Returning by Underburnmouth again about a mile from Newcastleton we stopped to examine the " Millholm Cross " which stands in a railed enclosure in a field above the road, and just about opposite the ruins of Mangerton Castle seen across fields beside the Liddel. Tradition says it marks the spot where the body of the Laird of Mangerton, who had been decoyed to Hermitage by either Lord Soulis or Angus and murdered, was rested by his men on the return to Mangerton.

Of these powerful Mangerton lairds there is a strange postscript given in a report by Lord Scrope to Walsingham in January 1583:

Regarding the revenge on the Liddesdales, I have so dealt that on Frydaye morninge laste Humfrey Musgrave, my deputie, Henry Leighe, stewarde of Brughe, with Captain Pickman and the souldiouris . . . have taken the Larde Mangerton in his owne house. . . . This man is chief and principal of his surname, and also special evildoer, and procurer be the spoile of the Marches, next after the laird of Wheathaugh, whom though I cannot well come bye, yet I hope in tyme to grieve both him and his. . . . His taking is greatly wondered at here, for it was never heard of that a laird of Mangerton was taken in his own house either in peace or war without the hurt or loss of a man.

At Newcastleton the railway line, which also cuts through Mangerton Castle, runs completely over the site of the pele of Jock Elliot of the Parke, who wounded Bothwell.

At this point we could have taken the Tarras Moss road, but remembering my experience of a year before I decided not to involve another driver. I had taken a cousin from England over that road then. We had been warned that it was a very treacherous road, but that it was in the process of re-surfacing. But Ella was determined to traverse the notorious Tarras Moss, and she said afterwards she would not have missed it for anything. Drained as it is now, and cleared of the concealing scrub, it yet had a sense of hidden menace. We were in the wildest part of the wild Border country, the fringe of which I had touched at the hound trails, and the view from the highest point of the Moss over that wild waste was indeed awe-inspiring.

At Newcastleton we were leaving the country of the Armstrongs for that of the Elliots, though here they overlap, for beyond the town Wheathaugh of the Armstrongs and Larriston of the Elliots are close together.

" New " Castleton was a creation of the Duke of Buccleuch in 1793 to house a colony of weavers. Today it is the centre of the hill-sheep country, its great day being the old " Copshawholm " Agricultural Show.

About a mile outside Newcastleton we noticed the farm of Roan, the site of the old tower of Redheugh of the Elliot clan. Some old carved stones incorporated in the walls of garden and steading are probably relics of the tower.

By the bridge that spans the Hermitage Water where it is just about to enter the Liddel the road branches left to Hawick and right to Jedburgh. We took the right turn up the steep brae to the site of Liddel Castle and the old hamlet of Castleton covered mostly now by a burying ground. Outside the graveyard walls the lines of the old settlement can still be traced, but there is not a stone of the castle left. The earthwork is quite apparent, however, above a precipice sheer to the Liddel, which takes a wide curve round its base. A more imposingly defensive site is this, Lord Soulis's first castle, than the later one of Hermitage. David I, on his return from captivity in England, gave to Randulph de Sules, who had come up with him, the barony of Liddesdale, and it seems to have remained with the Soulis family until the late thirteenth century.

Edward I stayed a night here on his journey from Roxburgh Castle to Liddesdale in 1296.

But we must hurry now. Hermitage and the Elliot country must wait. The short November day was closing in. It had not actually rained, but it had been a uniformly grey day. But now as we sped over Swinney Moor the sky had begun to lighten. As I looked back the western sky was layered with bars of pale to deep gold: ahead it was feathered thickly with wisps of pink cloud, and beneath, on all sides of the ribbon of grey road, the acres of bracken were aflame. We seemed caught up in a world of glowing colour —above, beneath, around. That alone was sufficient recompense for a November day's outing.

VI

Hermitage and Rule Waters

THE ROUTE we had taken the previous day out of Liddesdale was by Note-o-the Gate to Jedburgh—the route Scott would take with Shortreed, the Sheriff-Substitute of Roxburgh whom he had first met at Jedburgh. It was a well-known passage-way in the western Cheviots between Liddesdale and Carter Bar, rising at one point to 1200 feet.

Saughtree lies at its foot, about nine miles from Newcastleton, and a road branches south and follows the Liddel to near its source at Deadwater station. Here, near a section of the Catrail, the Border line is crossed, the North Tyne rises in marshy ground, and the road follows its course through Kielder Forest to Falstone, and on by Bellingham and Wark to Chollerford and the Roman Wall. It is still one of the quieter roads over the Border and one of the most beautiful.

Scott made a " raid " in seven successive years into Liddesdale with Shortreed, " exploring every rivulet to its source and every ruined Peel from foundation to battlement." On one of the very first they discovered an Elliot who played to them " on his Border Pipe " the real " lilt " of Dick o' the Cow.

" He was makin' himsell a' the time," remarked Shortreed, " but he didna ken maybe what he was about till years had passed; at first he thought little, I daresay, but the queerness and the fun."

" Eh me," continues Shortreed, " sic an endless fund o' humour and drollery as he then had wi' him. Never ten yards but we were either laughing or roaring or singing." Out of these days of sheer unadulterated enjoyment were born the *Minstrelsy of the Scottish Borders*, and his own first " Lays " and Border novels. There was a time when Scott hankered to be an artist, and one of his first sketches was of Hermitage—made standing up to his middle in snow for over an hour—a sketch that became the foundation on

F [69]

which another artist worked for an illustration for the first edition of the *Minstrelsy*.

Nevertheless I had never had much urge to visit Hermitage. In photographs it looked so massive, so solid, and it has the darkest and grimmest history of any Border keep. The murder of the Cout o' Kielder by Lord Soulis, and his own barbarous end at the hands of his oppressed tenants; the cruel death by slow starvation of Dalhousie by the Douglas, "Dark Knight of Liddesdale"; the tragedy of Mary Queen of Scots' visit to her wounded Warden, Bothwell, and its fateful consequences—legend and history alike make up its dark story.

I shall never forget my first sight of Hermitage. I had approached it in a friend's car by way of the wild pass of Mosspaul. All the way my eyes had been on these awesome hills above the narrow pass. I saw the terrible path down which Mary Queen of Scots rode on that bright October day that turned to wild weather—over thirty miles each way—after nearly coming to her death when her palfrey stumbled on Priesthaugh Swire—still called the "Queen's Mire." A little silver spur was found there many years ago.

Then, past Gorrenbury, my eyes had been drawn down to the lightly wooded banks of Hermitage Water running close to the road, a lovely stream. Suddenly the car rounded a bend into open country and I raised my eyes to the bare hillside, and there it was —Hermitage Castle, grey and ghostly, ethereal, like a ghost out of the past.

When we got close to it I saw it for what it was—"the most perfect of the medieval castles in the Scottish Borders," as the Roxburgh volume of Ancient Monuments says.

Though it does not look in a particularly defensive position for a fortress only five miles from the Border on Larriston Fells, it was earlier surrounded by miles of bog "the Hermitage Slack." The present castle is believed to be largely as reconstructed by Dacre while he was in possession, having got it by marrying the widow of the "Dark Knight." Like every other Border castle it changed hands many times. When it had passed to Bothwell, fourth Earl, Mary Queen of Scots made him a Warden of the Marches and Keeper of Liddesdale. He it was who had gone to France to bring her back to Scotland in 1561—and married her in 1567.

It was while he was attempting to arrest the reiver Jock Elliot of the Parke on 7 October 1566 that Bothwell was seriously wounded. On 17 October Mary, who was attending a justice court at Jedburgh, rode to Hermitage—not by Note-o-the Gate, but from Hawick through the Buccleuch country which was friendly to her.

Leyden's ballad " Lord Soulis " is not particularly good, and Bartram's Dirge, accepted by Scott as genuine, is believed to be Surtees' own. The only ballad connected with Hermitage now accepted as genuine is " Little Jock Elliot." The refrain is the Border slogan:

> Wha daur meddle wi' me?
> Wha daur meddle wi' me?
> My name is little Jock Elliot
> And wha daur meddle wi' me?

It was the Cout o' Kielder's grave we had come to find.

Of the traditional grave—a mound measuring eleven feet in length—the Roxburgh book of Ancient Monuments says: " This may be the grave of Sir Richard Knout (Knut) of Kielder in Tynedale, Sheriff of Northumberland who died 1289–91."

We found the grave on the banks of the Hermitage, a little to the west of the castle beside the ruins of the old chapel. The Hermitage at this point widens to make a pool, where the Cout is said to have been drowned. The Cout was the keen adversary of the Lord Soulis of his day. Traditionally, and as described in Leyden's ballad, he was lured to Hermitage. Realising his peril, he fled from the supper table, but on crossing the pool he stumbled and was handicapped by his armour in rising. He was set on and held down till he drowned.

Leyden's other ballad is concerned with the traditionally grisly end of the Lord Soulis who, in the time of Bruce, so oppressed his tenants (and who was also accused of sorcery) that they were continually appealing to the King for redress. Getting tired of their constant complaints the King is said to have exclaimed impatiently: " Oh, go boil him if you like, but don't let me hear of him again! " And that they did—in a cauldron hung between two of the " druidical " stones on the Nine-Stane-Rig.

That is legend. But there seems considerable historical ground for believing that the Borderers were encouraged in their lawlessness by the consistent neglect of their kings, and that they did have some desire for rule and order.

There is a letter (quoted in the *Calendar of Border Papers*) from Foster the English Warden to Walsingham, in 1584:

> In reply to your letter of the 2ᵈ instant, signifying the Council's desire to know on what ground the assurance is taken with the principal inhabitants of the opposite marches—seeing I could get no redress for these ten years from king, council, or Warden, and that the offer came from themselves, I thought it for Her Majesty's honour and quietness of her subjects to have taken it only till the first week in Lent next, though they desired to have the assurance longer which I refused till I knew Her Majesty's pleasure. . . . No like offer was ever made by such people to a Warden, and if ever I did Her Majesty any service this was one.

Then follows the assurance—" made at the Harmytage Castell 18th December 1584," the list of subscribers being headed by the chiefs of the Elliot clan of " Readhewgate," and the Armstrong of " Whithawhis " and " Mangerston," including the Laird's Jock, with the lesser clans of Nixone and Croser.

The Castle's history entered a more settled period under the Buccleuchs, and in 1930 (the fifth duke having already restored it extensively in the mid-nineteenth century) it was handed over to the Ministry of Works.

We had just time to find the Nine-Stane-Rig, generally considered to be the ancient Dexa-stane, which lay somewhere between the Dawstane Burn and the Slitrig road to Hawick. Passing Hermitage farm, Bobbie parked the car at the second bridge over the Whitterhope Burn on the Slitrig road. On the right bank of the burn we started up a gully and came out on what looked like acres of knee-high bent rising gradually to the long 943 ft ridge. It was treacherous going, with patches of bog. I sighed for a sure-footed Border garron—and I could have got one at the Crown Inn at Langholm, which is now a centre for " trail riding." I wondered, too, why the peasants had chosen this particular height to boil Lord Soulis—perhaps they were mounted! Was it some atavistic impulse that led them to the " stanes " where their ancestors had carried out their pagan rites?

At last Bobbie, who had forged on ahead, signalled that he had sighted the stone circle. Only two leaning stones showed above the bent. As usual, local people had believed these stones to be monuments of a great battle of which they were still dimly aware. But these stones were there before ever history was written.

In the year 603:

Aidan, King of Scots, who dwelt in Britain came against Aethelfrith, King of Northumberland, with an immense army, but beaten, he fled away with few. For in a very renowned place called Dexa stane . . . all his army was slain.

(Chronicle of Holyrood)

In this battle it was the Saxon pagan hosts which were victorious over the Christian Scottish King Aidan. It is referred to by other early annalists, and Fordun quotes Bede: " after this no King of Scots durst come to make war on the Angles to this day." It was to have a decisive effect on Scottish history. Aethelfrith's victory split the old British kingdom of Strathclyde, driving a wedge between the Britons of Strathclyde and the Britons of Wales.

As we came down the hillside and gained the car again the great dragging clouds that had been gathering over Liddesdale broke in a heavy deluge. The hills were blotted out. On such a day Queen Mary had ridden to Hermitage.

The Elliots had ruled the upper Liddel Valley as the Armstrongs had the lower. The Armstrongs spread westward into Eskdale and Ewesdale, but the Elliots moved eastward up the Slitrig, the Rule and Teviot.

Happily the Elliots, cradled in wild Liddesdale with the Armstrongs, have survived the disorder of these times, and since the days of " Gibbie o' the Gowden Garters " have given some of the most distinguished names in later Scottish history: Lord Heathfield, defender of Gibraltar; the first Earl Minto, Viceroy of India; the second Earl, Ambassador, First Lord of the Admiralty, and Lord Privy Seal; and in our own time, the Hon. Walter Elliot, perhaps the best-loved Borderer since Sir Walter Scott of Abbotsford—loved for the same qualities of heart and mind, his power of intellect, his humility, his wide humanity and devotion to the Borderland.

And Jean Elliot of Minto will always be remembered for her ballad version of the " Flowers of the Forest."

One historian ventures the opinion that the Elliots were im-
ported wholesale from Angus to the Borders to bolster the
waning power of the Douglas. John Buchan, however, considered
that the Elwalds (as they were first known) were indigenous: " the
same race as other septs of Liddesdale . . . deriving descent from
blood mixed with ancient Norse rovers and Britons of Strathclyde."

The Elliots were certainly squires of the Red Douglas. In 1476
Archibald, Earl of Douglas (" Bell-the-Cat "), as Lord of Liddesdale granted a charter of lands to " our well belufit fameliar
squiar, Robert Elwald of ye Redheuch, for his gude and faithful
servis to us don and to be don."

Larriston seems to have superseded Redheugh as stronghold.
Later Stobs came into the possession of a cadet of Larriston and
became the most important property. This Elliot was, however,
not acknowledged as chief. His to-name was " Gibbie o' the
Gowden Garters," from which it would appear he had expensive
tastes. He married a daughter of " Auld Wat o' Harden " and
" the Flower of Yarrow," and her to-name was " Maggie
Fendy." " Fendy " in Scots means " good at making do," which
suggests a piquant marital combination.

We had passed Stobs on our way back from the Nine-Stane-Rig,
but Gibbie's tower is no more, and the estates were sold to the
Government in 1903 for a military camp.

Gibbie o' the Gowden Garters and Maggie Fendy had six sons,
the eldest of whom married a Douglas of Cavers. His son was the
first baronet of Stobs; but it was the fourth son, Gavin, the laird of
Midlem Mill, from whom the Elliots of Minto are descended.
Gavin Elliot was a laird, but he followed the calling of a miller and
was proud of it. He had no tower, but a small thatched cottage by
his mill stream, the Ale. No completer break could have been
made with the restless roving past. Perhaps Maggie Fendy
decided that. There were to be no more " lions of Liddesdale."

Gavin married into the legal profession, for his wife was the
daughter of a W.S. and sister of an advocate. They had two sons.
Robert, the eldest, inherited the mill and other property; but
Gilbert, " the younger son of a younger son," was a true " Fendy."

He began as a lawyer in Edinburgh and had he conformed to the
government of his day he might have led an uneventful life. But—
was it here that the old freebooting strain asserted itself?—his
sympathies were all with the hunted Covenanters. As a result he

became one of the hunted. He had saved the life of the Earl of Argyll, who was imprisoned in Edinburgh Castle, by outstripping the King's messenger from London bearing the death warrant. The Earl escaped disguised as a page carrying the train of his stepdaughter, the Lady Sophia Lindsay, and reached the safety of Northumberland—the refuge of many a Scots Covenanter. Gilbert Elliot, like Hume of Marchmont, was suspected of being involved in the Ryehouse Plot, and the fortunes of the two fugitive men were almost identical: concealment and escape to Holland, long exile, return at the Revolution and final reinstatement with honours. In 1692 he was knighted, in 1700 created a baronet, and in 1703 he bought the estate of Minto, where as a boy he had spent happy holidays with his aunt, the wife of Turnbull of Minto. He was a member of the Scots Parliament which met to consider the Union of Parliaments, and, though not opposed to Union, voted against some of the principles, and was against the abolition of the Scots legislature.

Robert of Midlem never rose to higher rank than J.P., and although he was willing to " factor " the Minto estates, he never forgot he was the eldest son. He was never " Lord Minto's brother ": " Na, na," he would say, " Gibbie's *my* brother." He married Elizabeth Elliot, a daughter of Henry Elliot of Harwood.

Harwood, anciently Harrot-on-Rule, still belongs to the Elliot family. Their first charter is dated 1637. It was the home of Walter Elliot, and is the home of his widow, now Baroness Elliot.

Harwood lies up the Rule Water Valley in the lee of the great Wyndburg hill. A burn comes down through a beautiful wooded ravine and skirts the lawn. The hills are behind and before. For two busy people, immersed in national affairs, yet country-lovers and Borderers at heart, I could think of no happier retreat.

Of Harwood tower there is no trace, but a carved stone built into the stable may have come from it. At the door of the present house lies a part of a cross-head of red sandstone, found in the foundations of the decayed Appotsyde House. This may have been from a cross standing by one of the old roads.

Facing the house is Bonchester Hill, crowned by one of the most notable of the prehistoric forts.

Although Rule Water received the Elliots, it was mainly Turnbull country:

Where Turnbulls once, a race no power could awe
Lined the rough skirts of stormy Ruberslaw.

The Turnbulls gave more trouble to the Stuart kings than perhaps any other clan except the Armstrongs. Indeed an order went
out: " Hang every tenth Turnbull," and the Deadhaugh at
Spittal-on-Rule is said to record that it was done.

Boece, Fordun's " Continuator," seems to be responsible for the
traditional origin of the Border Turnbulls, and it has long been
current in the Borders. One William de Roulle saved Bruce's life
from a ferocious bull by seizing it by the horns and throwing it to
the ground, and for this rescue he was given lands in the
Borders and became known as Turne-e-bull. So much for the
Border tradition. The bull's head appears on various crests.
Turnbull of Bedrule's crest was a bull's head in half profile and the
motto " I saved the King "; while Turnbull of Mynto has no
motto and the bull's head faces front.

But it is to be noted that there was a Norman family of the name
of Tournebu in France in the thirteenth century and it has been
asserted that the Turnbull cast of features is distinctly Norman!
In a book *Les Ecossais en France, les Français en Ecosse* by Francisque-
Michel the Tournebulles, whose arms were silver with a blue band
and three black bulls' heads, are among several families mentioned
as having come to France from Scotland.

The first documentary reference to the Border Turnbulls is
apparently in 1357, when an Adam de Roule resigned his lands in
Altownburn and they passed into the hands of John Ker of the
forest of Ettrick.

The Border Turnbulls were at their zenith of power in the late
fifteenth century, their chief's stronghold being Bedrule Castle.
At one time they held all the Rule Water Valley from source to
Teviot, and on the north bank of Teviot the lands of Minto,
Hassendeanbank, Standhill, Barnhill, Rowflat, Belses and Bewlie
—names which were to appear later in Covenanting annals, for,
as the Rev. Duncan Stewart says, in his *Covenanters of Teviotdale*,
" The most frequent Covenanting name in Teviotdale was
Turnbull "—as, it may be added, it had been in Pitcairn's
Criminal Trials!

Among the " hottest " (Surrey's word) reivers they seemed to
have been particularly offensive to the English Wardens.

According to a family historian:

> In 1545 the English burned 12 Castles and forts in the valley of Rule with the towers of Mynto, Mynto Crags and Barnhill. They at the same time plundered the clan of almost the whole of their cattle and other means of subsistence, . . . killing and making many of them prisoners. . . . The Turnbulls as well as most of the Borderers were coerced into taking assurance under the English. They were furnished with the crosses of St George and compelled to accompany the English army in their ravages. But when the Scots met the English on Ancrum Moor, the Turnbulls and others seized their opportunity to throw away their red crosses and turn their swords against their real foes . . . they shewed as little mercy as they had received.

This question of " assurance " is a tricky one. But there is no doubt many of the Borderers were forced into it. Equally, with both English and Scottish Borderers, such shifts were looked on as necessary temporary measures. The English monarchs had as little cause to trust their own " fell men " when it came to taking them over the Border.

In 1573 Sir Andrew Turnbull of Bedrule led his clan in the raid of the Reidswire. In 1586 an Act was passed for " the putting down of thieves in the Borders," and the Laird of Bedrule appears in the list of " broken men." But gradually, step by step, some kind of order began to emerge. In 1591 Bedrule's name appears in a bond subscribed by most of the barons in the East March to support James VI: in 1593 the chiefs of clans were bound to give pledges to keep the peace, and finally in 1606 it was commanded " all armour to be put away."

But the unruly clan was still to give trouble to constituted authority; even in such small matters as encounters with the local Presbytery. The ancient right of " burying in the kirk " was now frowned on, but the Turnbulls are on record as " breaking into the kirk to bury there-in," and when the Presbytery refused permission to George Turnbull to marry Kirstane Turnbull " because of his slanderous life and living without any calling " a later entry has to record " Leave granted." A Nicola Turnbull, daughter of the Laird of Bedrule, showed no less spirit in 1632 by running away with the Minister's assistant.

In 1662 Lord Linton (son of the Earl of Traquair a favourite of Charles I) with a hundred men plundered Bedrule " carrying off even the Minister's corn." The Turnbulls were now on the side of the rebellious Covenanters and were, with the Elliots, suffering fines and forfeiture. Turnbull of Mynto's wife and the Lady of Stobs were sisters in adversity.

But it was still in mosstrooping times that this turbulent clan produced its brightest offshoot: William Turnbull of the Bedrule family, born about 1400. He was the founder, and later Chancellor, of Glasgow University.

On 5 January 1951, the fifth centenary celebrations of Glasgow University were inaugurated at Bedrule. After a service in the Kirk, Colonel Bruce Turnbull, as representative of the Bedrule Turnbulls, lit a bonfire from which Mr Walter Elliot, Rector of the University 1947–50, handed a burning torch which was relayed by student runners to Glasgow.

" Also present," as the phrase goes, was Sir Hugh Turnbull, Commissioner of the London Metropolitan Police.

VII

Teviotdale

THERE IS NO mistaking that Hawick is an industrial town. Selkirk, Galashiels, Langholm, Jedburgh, Peebles—the larger of the Border mill towns—have all the air of a country town, but in Hawick factory chimneys predominate, the houses are more tightly packed, the traffic is heavier.

Yet, in this hive of industry, in the long High Street which is in the very heart of the town, is set one lone statue—the figure of a Border warrior on a pawing steed, holding high a battle pennon.

Now this is completely symbolic of Hawick—nowhere else perhaps is the Border frontier spirit stronger than in the heart of a " Teri." On Common Riding Day an uninitiated, astonished visitor might well think this industrial town had gone mad—the factory lads and lasses parading the streets, and cheering on a band of youths on horseback, one bearing a banner.

To answer the question—" What is it all about ? " would take more than one chapter to do it justice.

It would mean telling a story that goes back to " fable-shaded eras "; of an Anglo-Saxon settlement; a mysterious mote hill; and a phrase that is older than any ballad; of a continually harassed frontier town; of the sturdy defence by the burgesses of their common rights; of Flodden.

One does not normally expect to find history and romance in the main street of an industrial town. Nevertheless the first evening of my stay in Hawick I walked down the High Street, starting at the statue, which is universally and familiarly known as " the Horse." It is obvious that this is a mosstroopers' town. Writing of the Border festivals in *Knowing Scotland* John Mackay has hit on their salient feature:

It is the horse that helped to make the " brave Borderland " that much different from the rest of Scotland and it still *is* the horse who can lift one's heart at the sight of a living frieze of them on a moorland brow.

This statue commemorates an incident after Flodden. Hawick's contingent, like Selkirk's, was practically exterminated at Flodden. Sir William Douglas of Drumlanrig was the leader, and he, with 200 Douglases, was killed. With him, and Sir Walter Scott of Branxholme, were the clans of Elliot, Turnbull, Crozier, Rutherford, etc. Sir Walter Scott was one of the few who escaped.

The English army did not follow up their victory and secure the country—for what reasons became clearer to me when I reached Flodden Field—but a year after the battle Dacre was still in the Borders. In a letter of May 1514 he gives an account of a raid along Ewes to Carlanrig, and from the headwater of Teviot down into Branxholme " all every one of them wasted now and no corn sowne upon none of said ground." But though he circled round he did not advance on Hawick. It was probably one of his marauding bands that was sighted at Hornshole, about two miles out of Hawick. Two hundred of the youth of the town (" callants," many of them who had been too young to fight at Flodden) set out and routed the English, capturing their flag. This flag was a pennon emblazoned with a gold cross on a blue ground with the arms of the Priory of St Andrew of Hexham, and its replica is carried at the Common Riding by the Cornet, who must always be an unmarried " callant."

At the end of the High Street proper is the Tower Hotel, which has still some of the original walls of the Black Tower of the Douglas, and which later belonged to the Scotts of Buccleuch. It survived the many burnings when the thatched " biggings " of the town were set on fire either by the enemy or the people themselves to smoke out the invader while they themselves took to the hills. (Branxholme was so burned by Buccleuch.)

The first feudal lords of Hawick seem to have been the Lovels —(Lufellus, " Little wolf ") who were lords of Yvery in Normandy, and Somerset in Northumberland. Their allegience was to England and this eventually cost them their inheritance in Scotland. Balliols, Cumyns, Murrays, Douglases, and Scotts successively became overlords.

In 1773 it was converted into an inn. Dorothy and William Wordsworth put up for a night there on their Border tour, coming with Scott from Jedburgh. Dorothy noted the thickness of the walls, " about a yard." Next day Scott took them to the top of the Vertish Hill, where Dorothy was impressed by the wonderful ranges of the hills. Today the Hawick people speak lovingly of their town as " Hawick among the hills."

Just beyond the tower, I climbed some steps to St Mary's Kirk, round which the life of Hawick—religious, political and commercial—has revolved for centuries; the very precincts of the church serving for local parliamentary meetings, justice courts, and military barracks. How old the first foundation was is uncertain but a church on this site was dedicated by the Bishop of Caithness 1214. St Cuthbert had a chapel further up the Slitrig, and the first documentary reference to Hawick is in connexion with this chapel in Reginald of Durham's twelfth-century Book of St Cuthbert.

The memorial gates giving on the churchyard commemorate the granting of Hawick's charter by Sir James Douglas of Drumlanrig in 1537. He succeeded his father who fell at Flodden; he was with Buccleuch in the attempted rescue of young James V at the battle of Melrose, and was a Warden of the West March. St Mary's for nearly two centuries was the burial place of the Scotts of Buccleuch, including the Bold Buccleuch. But the " common man " has also his monument: " ane honeste man Johne Dennis, tenent kyndlie of Havick Miln and slain in debait [defence] of his nichtborris [neighbours] gier 1546."

Within St Mary's Kirk in 1342 was staged that dramatic scene when the " dark knight of Liddesdale " broke into the justice court over which Sir Alexander Ramsay of Dalhousie was presiding. (Jedburgh, at that time, was occupied by the English.) The two rivals faced each other. They had been comrades in arms and both had served their king faithfully. Douglas had rid all Teviotdale of the English but had failed to take Roxburgh Castle. Dalhousie had succeeded where he had failed and the King had preferred him over Douglas. Dalhousie was seized by Douglas and dragged from the kirk to the dungeon of Hermitage.

A little further on I arrived at the " Mote." It is a grass-grown mound, perfectly round and smooth in outline, 30 feet high and 312 feet in circumference at the base. Doubts exist whether or not it was a site of pagan rites—" where Druid shades still flitted round " (Scott); meeting place of the Saxons; or tumulus, or foundation of British fort. The Hawick Cornet, however, wearing his druidical oak leaves, leads the dancers from the Common Riding ball to the top of the Mote to greet the rising sun, and sing " Teribus " once more.

Was that curious refrain, which comes into the Common Riding Song like the " owre-word " of a ballad, originally—as Professor Murray suggests—" a relic of North Anglian heathendom: ' Tyr-ibus ye Tyr ye Odin! Tyr haeb us, Tyr ye Odin!' —Tyr keep us, both Tyr and Odin "?

Every step I had taken that evening had been a step farther back into the past. From the statue to the tower had been several centuries back to the beginning of feudalism; to the church was to the dawn of Christianity in the Borders; and now I stood on the top of a mysterious great mound about which no one could confidently say he knew anything at all.

Later I walked down the Slitrig, which flows past the Mote, to the high water mark on the wall that records the height of the flood of 1767. It was above my head level. There was some meaning in Leyden's " Hawick shall triumph over flame and flood." In his *Scenes of Infancy* he records the legend of the small deep lake on top of Wyndburgh inhabited by the spirit of the mountain. To disturb the waters by throwing stones was considered offensive. When the Slitrig on 5 August 1767,

> rose to uncommon height, without extraordinary rain falling that day, or some days before, and the River Teviot was then fordable . . . 15 dwelling houses, with corn mill at the end of the town presently swept away,
>
> *(Annals of Hawick)*

superstitious fears were aroused, but, above the flood, the minister called the people to prayer in St Mary's Kirk. No lives were lost, not even that of a servant girl who waded through the swirling waters to retrieve a bag of £300 in gold her master had in the house, and on returning was swept down with the flood and cast up on a bank below the town, still clutching the money bag.

Crossing the Slitrig where it enters Teviot I wandered through Wilton Park—a natural unspoiled stretch of Teviot—the inspired purchase of the town fathers.

Within the grounds near the mansion house, now the museum, a stone marks the site of the thorn tree where Wallace is said to have tethered his horse. Probably he was on his way into Northumberland when he stopped to visit his friend Longueville (Langlands).

The museum is a perfect epitome of Border history from Mesolithic to late Victorian. Among a collection of flints, collected mostly in the Merse of the East March, Professor Gordon Childe made the exciting discovery of one rare specimen of microhirum—a small implement " typical product of the oldest human industry yet found in Scotland that flourished in the Mesolithic phase between the stone age and the bronze age, over 4,000 years ago."

But the item which interested me most was a unique carved stone family tree dated 1690. Here were shown the Rutherfords of that ilk and their intermarriages with Riddells, Elliots of Larriston, Douglas, Murray, Ramsay, Home, Nisbet, etc.—all names in Border ballad and story.

The " bauld Rutherfords " have more than one traditional origin for their name, both connected with a ford. " Rudderford " the red ford on Tweed is one; the other is that they were so named for taking an ancient king " Ruther " safely through a river. Historically, their name occurs in a charter of William the Lion in 1165. A Rutherford rallied to Wallace with sixty men, while his son supported Bruce. In 1398 a Richard de Rutherford was an Ambassador to England and in 1400 one of the Wardens of the Marches. They will be met with in " The Raid of the Reidswire."

It had been December when I reached Hawick on my journey along the Border line, but I had already seen the Common Riding.

Hawick, Selkirk, and Langholm are the oldest Border Common Ridings. A record of the list of Hawick Cornets is unbroken from 1703 to 1914 when there was a lapse of four years, during which no Cornet was chosen owing to the War, and another from 1940 to 1945. But the perambulation of the Marches was never allowed to lapse.

The pattern of riding the boundaries is the same in these Common Ridings, but Hawick is unique in that women riders are banned. The Riding of the Marches is an entirely masculine concern, like one of the old riding ballads itself. The Cornet's chase up the Nipknowes is a furious affair, symbolic of the capture of the flag and pursuit.

But it would be a mistake to assume that women have a merely decorative part. The Cornet chooses his Lass—one might say she is the knight's " ladye gay." She has the important part in the " colour bussing " ceremony in the Town Hall on the eve of the Common Riding where she busses, *i.e.* decks or dresses, the flag with the Cornet's colours. She has her court which includes the " lass " of the Right Hand Man and that of the Left Hand Man, and a colourful bevy of maids of honour.

A distinguished guest is invited to give the " oration " and the standard demanded is high. In 1961 the speaker was Lord Polwarth, of Harden, descendant of " Auld Wat," and he also took part in the chase and riding of the marches.

Seating accommodation in the Town Hall is limited. Returned overseas exiles are given first place and competition for the remaining tickets is keen. For the Teri who is privileged to be there it is, as Lord Polwarth said, " the most stirring and solemn moment of the Common Riding."

Hawick may have no ballad—unless it can claim " Jamie Telfer "—but its Common Riding Song " Teribus " is set to an old air, and everywhere there is singing: at the ride-outs; at the bussing ceremony; before the march-riders set out; at the various halts; at dawn on the Mote hill.

Unexpectedly, the moment that was to thrill me most was to come when I returned in May 1961 for the " Mosspaul Ride," one of the preliminary ride-outs before the Common Riding day and which I had not yet seen. The route is fourteen miles long, the last ten over the rough moorland heights about Mosspaul, and the riders must face whatever weather is going, wind, rain, or even snow in these heights. Some never win through. Those who do are awarded the coveted " mosstrooper's badge."

The riders start from the town at 1.30 and are expected down at Mosspaul about 4 p.m. Thanks to a Teri enthusiast with a car we got there in time to manoeuvre into a good position in the long line of cars that stretched for at least half a mile along the roadside. But we decided to leave the car and climb the hillside above the Frostlee Burn—remembering Johnie and his " gallant companie."

These moments of waiting are tense. Will all the riders get through? Will the Cornet be first? The clouds have gathered and are lowering. But they part. The sun comes out. We see the riders against the skyline. Their coloured jerkins make a motley in the sun. They come pouring down the hillside jesting and laughing, confident and sure as their horses. In that moment the mosstroopers lived again—the shades I had companioned with so long.

The crests of the Scotts of Buccleuch and the Scotts of Harden both bear the crescent moon and stars—witness of the days when they were " gentlemen of the shade, minions of the moon." Their strongholds lay close together, on either side of the Borthwick Water, a few miles from Hawick.

It was in the spring of 1567 that Wat o' Harden had married Mary Scott of Dryhope, " The Flower of Yarrow," and was pledged to bring his father-in-law the proceeds of the first moonlight raid. There is some doubt as to which was the first married home of Mary Scott, Kirkhope or Harden. But Will H. Ogilvie bases his ballad " Whaup o' the Rede " on Kirkhope.

It is now some years since I first visited Harden. About three miles up Borthwick Water a side road turns up on the right, and goes over the hills to Ashkirk, at this point entering the Harden Glen where Wat used to hide his stolen cattle. Their owners might pursue them " with hue and cry, with horse and hound," but if they could be held for a week and a day they became the property of the raider, by the law of the " Hot Trod."

It may be interesting to read how it appeared to a contemporary of the Borderer, John Lesley, Bishop of Ross:

> In time of war they are readily reduced to extreme poverty by the almost daily inroads of the enemy . . . whence it happens they seek their subsistence by robberies, or rather plunder and rapine (for they are particularly averse to the shedding of blood) nor do they much concern themselves whether it be from Scots or English that they rob. . . . They have a persuasion that all property is common by law of nature.

and he adds that they never said their prayers more fervently than before a raid. The blood feuds arose out of some insult or injury to a member of the clan.

Harden House stands at the head of the glen on the edge of a precipitous tree-clad cliff. The back of the house is now the main entrance. The south front has a narrow terrace, enclosed by a battlemented wall which falls sheer to the ravine.

G

That day I could see over the ravine clear to the hills that range all along the horizon. An advancing enemy would be clearly seen.

About Harden there are no parks, no well-ordered " policies," all is in a natural state. The trees rise up the side of the glen to the very wall of the terrace and on the rising hillsides behind. Above and beyond are the moors and heathery hills.

Within the house one room, which was the old kitchen but which is now the children's nursery, is thought to be the only remaining part of the original tower. It has a huge hearth fireplace on which logs were laid. Some modern toys scattered about did not, somehow, strike an incongruous note, rather a reassuring one that there was still young life in that old, old house—heirs to its glorious tradition.

Here I was reminded of the pathetic story of the little Mary, Countess of Buccleuch. She succeeded to the title when only four years old, and became, even more than usual in those days, a marriage pawn. The Earl of Tweeddale, her uncle, and Gideon Scott of Highchesters, second son of Sir William Scott of Harden, both desired a marriage with their sons. Her mother, now married to the Earl of Wemyss, favoured Highchesters. When Mary was just eleven years old, Walter Scott, the fourteen-year-old son of Highchesters, was kidnapped on his way to school at St Andrews and married to Mary in the Chapel of Wemyss in the presence of her trustees.

She was a frail, delicate child, " thoughtful beyond her years," and her tender little letters to her boy husband have been preserved. She died before she was fourteen, and young Highchesters, who had been created Earl of Tarras, received nothing of the Buccleuch inheritance. (He married again, and it was a descendant of this second marriage who successfully claimed the title of Baron Polwarth, through his mother, Diana Hume Campbell, in 1835.) The Countess of Wemyss next set about getting her remaining daughter, Anne, now the Countess of Buccleuch, married to the natural son of Charles II, created Duke of Monmouth. In accordance with her father's will he had to take the name of Scott. Dryden, Evelyn, Pepys, all wrote of the charm, wit and goodness of the young Scots girl, but her marriage too was to end in tragedy. She was the Duchess in Scott's *Lay of the Last Minstrel* who had " wept o'er Monmouth's bloody tomb."

From the house we motored up the hill road on the moors behind, and there, 1,000 feet up with the snell wind whistling in our ears, we looked over the Harden Glen, over the valleys of the Borthwick and Teviot to a very sea of hills from Carter Bar to the Cumberland Fells—the routes of the raiders lay plain before us. Never in all my Border wanderings have I had such a sense of desolate waste as looking out from above Harden. Yet it was beautiful, beautiful like the sea, like a "waste of waters," and, like it, responsive to the sky above.

Inevitably my thoughts went back to auld Wat o' Harden and the " riding ballads."

There is a tradition that a child was carried off inadvertently in a Northumberland raid, a bundle snatched up with other reiver's loot. On its discovery Wat o' Harden, unable to tell whose child it was, handed it over to the Flower of Yarrow to rear as one of her own sons. Tradition avers it was he who composed many of the ballads.

Leyden recalls the story:

> His are the strains, whose wandering echoes thrill
> The shepherd lingering on the twilight hill. . . .
> He, nameless as the race from which he sprung,
> Saved other names, and left his own unsung.

But to ask, Who wrote the ballads? is like asking Who wrote Shakespeare? or Who wrote Homer? and as controversial. Lewis Spence surmised that the ballads were " aristocratic . . . the production of a caste of highly skilled literary craftsmen." Quiller Couch hazards the guess "that hereabouts [the Borders], there lived a man of genius who gave these songs their immortal impress and taught it to others."

If I may be permitted a theory, there was a fraternity of minstrels, travelling the country and sometimes attached to particular clans. The English and Scottish ballads have so much in common —not only phrases but whole themes—that a minstrel would just take what suited his occasion.

However that may be, we know that legends travel the world by oral tradition: the same story appears in many guises in different countries. Arthur sleeps beneath many hills. In Yugoslavia he is the national hero under another name, and a tribe of American Indians have their Arthurian legend.

As I walked back to Hawick by the side of the Teviot the spring daylight was waning. Hawick townsfolk, untroubled by thoughts of foray and feud, were taking their evening stroll through Wilton Park.

Branxholme Hall was a magic name in my Border childhood, as it was to all of my generation. We all learned the *Lay* at school:

> Nine-and-twenty knights of fame
> Hung their shields in Branxholme Hall.

The Buccleuch Scotts were comparatively late comers to the Border line area, but they instantly made their mark. The name has its traditional origin, like so many others, in the exploit of a strong man. The story is that two Galloway brothers, banished, had come to Rankilburn in Ettrick and the Ranger of the Forest retained them " on account of their skill in winding the horn, etc." A King of Scots hunting in the Forest drove a powerful buck to bay on a ledge of a deep cleuch, which the dogs could not reach. One of the brothers got to close quarters, overthrew the buck, slung it across his shoulders, and carried it to the King. So he was dubbed " Buck's cleuch," and the crowned buck appears with the crescent and stars. This is Satchell's story in his rhymed history of the Scotts.

The known facts are that the Scotts first held lands in Scotstoun and Kirkurd in Peeblesshire.—Murthockston in Lanarkshire, was obtained by marriage to the heiress. Apparently the Laird of Murthockston obtained lands in Rankilburn, including Buccleuch, where their first tower stood and where probably their connexion with the forest ranger arose and led to the adoption of the buck crest. Their progress from Rankilburn over the hills by way of Bellenden on the high moors to Branxholme was by a series of exchanges and purchases.

By 1446 they were firmly established in Teviotdale, their tower on the Rankilburn falling into decay, and their House rose in power over the Douglases. By 1455 the Middle March was ruled by the Scotts of Buccleuch and Kers of Fernihirst and Cessford in turn: to Elizabeth, Cessford and Buccleuch were the " firebrands of the Borders."

When James VI went south to his new kingdom and proceeded

to wipe out the " Border line," the Bold Buccleuch did not fit into
the scheme of things. He gave up his duties as Governor of
Hermitage Castle, delegated his land to the management of the
Harden Scotts, and went to fight in Holland, taking 200 of his clan
with him and founding the second battalion of the Scots Regiment
of Holland.

The lands they left were now mostly waste—long ravished and
impoverished. Those who remained had to start from scratch.
Mosstrooping was no longer a gentlemanly occupation. Branxholme Tower had been put to the flames several times by the
English, but in 1570 when they were carrying fire and slaughter
through the Borders they found Branxholme " brynte to our hand
by hymselfe as cruelly as ourselves could have brynt yit . . . yit
was a very strong hous, and well sett, and very pleasant gardens
and orchards about yit, and well kept, but all destroyed."

Sir Walter Scott of Branxholme started the rebuilding in 1571,
but it was his widow, Lady Margaret Douglas, who completed it
in 1576. During modernisation much of the old castle was probably removed. Wordsworth's reaction on seeing it for the first
time was natural: " it looks better in your poem," he wrote to
Scott, " than in its present realities; the situation however is
delightful."

The Nelson Tower is now the oldest part of Branxholme Hall,
where Scott set the secret bower " that was guarded by word and by
spell, deadly to hear and deadly to tell." In the tower head he had
placed " Fair Margaret's bower " from which she stole to her
secret tryst with Cranston, enemy of the house. The day I
climbed to the little room at the top of the tower it was full of
spring sunlight. I looked down on the green meadow where the
Lists were held. Above were the hills which had carried the
beacons from " height to height." Teviot shone and sang in the
sun:

> As if thy waves, since time was born
>   Since first they rolled upon the Tweed
> Had only heard the shepherd's reed,
>   Nor started at the bugle horn.

But Border history, like Border scenery, is full of these changes of
mood. I was now about to pass into the country of the " Shepherd's reed."

Leyden's pastoral poem " Scenes of Infancy " is better than any of his ballads, but he was an indefatigable ballad-hunter and help to Scott in compiling the *Minstrelsy*. In him Scott found a man after his own heart—an enthusiast. Where Walter Scott rode thirty miles after one verse Leyden tramped forty miles there and back to obtain a ballad for Scott.

Denholm, where he was born, is an attractive village, about four miles from Hawick. The houses are set round a spacious green to form a square with Leyden's memorial in the centre. Some of the houses are old, but Leyden's birthplace is the only one now with a thatched roof. Although he was born here in September 1775, his father removed a year later to Henlawsteil to serve as a shepherd and there, at the base of Ruberslaw, Leyden grew up.

There is a curiously uniform pattern in the lives of our greater Border poets. All came of peasant or yeoman stock and their earliest formative years were spent on Border farms. Scott, although he was also descended from Harden lairds, had a farmer grandfather and was brought up as a child at Sandyknowe Farm. Thomson was the son of a gardener at Ednam, Leyden and Hogg were sons of shepherds. All owed their rearing in ballad and story to the distaff side, and they all wrote ballads.

Leyden became a great orientalist and died in Batavia on 28 August 1811. General Sir John Malcolm, the Eskdale knight, who knew him well, published a tribute to him in the *Bombay Courier* and then gives a picture of the old balladist:

> The love of the place of his nativity was a passion. I once went to see him when he was very ill. . . . He enquired if I had any news. I told him I had a letter from Eskdalemuir. " And what are they about in the Borders? " he asked. . . . I read him a passage which described the conduct of some of the volunteers on a fire being kindled by mistake at one of the beacons . . . the letter mentioned that the moment the blaze, which was the signal of invasion, was seen, the mountaineers hastened to their rendezvous and those of Liddesdale swam the Liddel river to reach it . . . at break of day the party reached the town of Hawick to the tune of " Wha daur meddle wi' me? " Leyden's countenance became animated as I proceeded . . . at its close he sprang from his sickbed and with strange melody . . . sung aloud " Wha daur meddle wi' me, Wha daur meddle wi' me."

Minto is only a few miles up from Denholm. By way of the lovely little village we came to Minto Crags and Fatlips Castle, which of all the Border peles came nearest to my idea of a robber baron's eyrie. It seemed particularly inaccessible today, for the late snow was still lying deep and paths in the woods that surround it were obliterated. But eventually we struck steps cut out in the crags, that ascend to the small level space on which the castle stands. It had been restored by the Minto family as a museum, and was closed. But Jean, my Teri cousin who had been taught the *Lay* at school and taught it at others, at my request stood on a crag and recited the familiar lines beginning:

> On Minto crags the moonbeams glint,
> Where Barnhill hewed his bed of flint . . .

Turnbull of Barnhill was the outlaw who found secure hiding place among the cliffs when his tower, lower down, was being searched. So did a Minto Elliot when he sought to evade an embarrassing meeting with Prince Charlie.

The crags themselves are 700 feet above sea level, and the view was reward enough for our climb. Ruberslaw looked very near, rising sheer from the valley and from this point a perfect cone, broad at the base and tapering at the top. Dunion stood out clearly, nearer to Jedburgh, and beyond were the Cheviots. Beneath us Teviot with many windings through a fair and fertile valley was on its way to join Tweed at Kelso. The wild ballad country ends here and the " Shepherd's reed " begins to take on the softer strain and pastoral songs of peasant love.

From the other side of the hill could be seen the Eildons, and the Minto hills, like a smaller replica without the third peak. In the vale lay Hassendean, where a few scattered stones mark the site of the ancient cell of Melrose Abbey and " where circles many a legendary tale "; lovely Lilliesleaf on whose Moss the Covenanters gathered and Turnbull of Standhill rode with Alexander Hume of the Merse, and where William Knox, the local poet, was born, and was inspired to write " O why should the spirit of mortal be proud," lines Abraham Lincoln quoted on the day he was assassinated.

We ended our day by wandering about the grounds of " Green Cavers hallowed by the Douglas name." We walked round the roofless house and the deserted garden, and thought we could trace the outlines of the older wall, embedded in the modern portion. The Norman Balliols owned it in the twelfth and thirteenth centuries before it became the tower of the Douglases, Wardens of the Middle March and Sheriffs of Teviotdale (one of whom was in the Reidswire raid). The founder of the Cavers branch was Archibald, the elder of the two natural sons of the Earl Douglas hero of Otterburn—the other being William, who founded Drumlanrig.

Among the last of the male line of Cavers was Sir William Douglas, who, for refusing to abjure the Covenant and failing to " compear " when summoned, was " put to the horn " and deprived of his sheriffdom.

VIII

Jed and Kale

O F ALL THE Abbey towns Jedburgh is the only one that seems to me to retain its medieval atmosphere. If you walk up the High Street you will see several " closes," and down the Canongate there are some fine rough-hewn or rubble stone sixteenth–seventeenth-century houses and at its foot a sixteenth-century bridge from which there is the best view of one of the few remaining bastel houses of the Borders—Queen Mary's House.

Jedburgh's recorded history goes back to 854 when Ecgred, Bishop of Lindisfarne, founded two settlements and called them Gedwearde—one later becoming the burgh. The Abbey, like all three others of David's founding, suffered burnings and sackings during Border warfare.

After the Reformation the Abbey passed to Sir Andrew Ker of Fernihirst, ancestor of the Marquis of Lothian, as Kelso did to Sir Robert Ker of Cessford, ancestor of the Duke of Roxburghe. It had been the ancestral burying-place of the Fernihirst Kers, and there were laid the ashes of the much loved Philip Ker, twelfth Marquis of Lothian, who has been termed the best ambassador Britain ever sent to America. In 1913 it was given into care of the Ministry of Works.

According to Surrey, the Abbey was as stoutly defended by the monks and burgesses of Jedburgh as was Kelso Abbey. It was after the assault on Jedburgh that he wrote in a letter to Henry VIII: " I assure your grace I found the Scottes, at this tyme, the boldest men, and the hotest, that ever I saw in any nation."

The castle was finally levelled in 1409 by the Scots themselves, for like all the Scots Border castles it had proved of more use to the enemy.

Yet, in times of peace, the castle was a kingly residence. It was one of the " hostages " for William the Lion at the Treaty of Falaise; Malcolm the Maiden died there; it was a marriage settlement on Joanna, sister of Henry III of England, on her marriage to Alexander II; and after Alexander III married, in the Abbey, Jolande, daughter of the Count of Dreux, as his second wife, a great feast and masque was held in the castle.

Jedburgh may be said to be famous for four things: the Jeddart Staff (prominent in Border warfare); Jeddart justice (hang them first and try them afterwards); Jeddart pears (a small, very sweet variety, descendants of the trees planted by the Abbey brethren); and the slogan " Jeddart's here! "

Being less than ten miles from the frontier the burgesses were trained for instant defence. Over 400 men were always ready for battle; the crafts alone provided 100. Jedburgh weavers fought at Bannockburn and brought home a flag, but it was burned in 1898. A coloured sketch of it is to be seen, with other relics, in Queen Mary's House.

Except when the English were in possession the justice courts were held in Jedburgh. James IV and James V came here with large forces to " put down the Borderers," and it was to Jedburgh that 200 of the Turnbull clan were brought, each with a halter round his neck. It was to hold a justice court that Queen Mary came to Jedburgh, and her defenders maintain that she did not ride to Hermitage until it was finished. She was so long ill with a fever afterwards that when she rode out of Jedburgh Bothwell was in her retinue. " Would God I had died at Jeddart," was her bitter cry in later years.

Jedburgh's slogan brings us to the last of the riding ballads, " The Raid of the Reidswire," and also one of the last of the frays at Wardens' meetings, when, according to a fragment of another ballad:

> *a*Bauld Rutherford, he was fu' stout,   *a bold*
> Wi' a' his nine sons him round about
> He led the town o' Jedburgh out.

On 7 June 1575 the Warden's court met at the Reidswire on the Border line just off the present road at Carter Bar. The Scottish Warden was Sir John Carmichael, the English was Sir John Foster. The ballad has not the terseness of the best riding ballads, but it is valuable as a roll-call of the Border clans. Carmichael, the Laird's Wat, the Armstrongs, the Elliots, the Douglases,

Cranstons, Gladstones, Turnbulls, Rutherfords, and " other clans " are all mentioned. Among famous Northumberland families mentioned are Heron of Chipchase, Fenwick of Wallington, Russel, Collingwood, and others.

The Scots " fyled " a bill against a notorious English fugitive, Farnstein, but Foster maintained he was " fled." Carmichael considered this an excuse for not paying compensation, and hot words ensued, but according to the ballad it was the Tynedale followers who actually started the fray, and the Scots were getting the worst of it when a party from Jedburgh suddenly appeared: " Fy, Tindaill to it! Jedburgh's here! "

This ballad appears in the *Minstrelsy*, but is not included in Child's collection.

You can wander about Jedburgh and be reminded of many famous Jedburgh characters: Sir David Brewster, son of the Master of the Grammar School; two scholars of that school, Samuel Rutherford and James Thomson; Mary Fairfax, later Somerville, who was born in the manse of her uncle, the local historian.

A tablet marks the lodgings in the Bow where Dorothy and William stayed while Scott was attending the courts, and where he read them parts of his still unpublished *Lay*; another in the Castlegate, where Prince Charlie halted on his march into England. As in Kelso he got little support. The spirit of the moss-troopers waited for another day—and it came on the night of the false alarm. Then the men of the hills and glens joined the Burgess in the light of flaming torches and houses were all lit up. Did the Jeddart Staff reappear that night?

On a neutral January day that seemed unable to decide between sun and snow I set out to walk to Fernihirst. Now, when winter has swept the country bare of foliage one makes fresh discoveries. Even the distant landscape stands revealed as never before. The day might be grey but the country would not be drab—I would leave that to town pavements and house walls. I would find plenty of colour in the fields, green by the river haughs; russet on the hillsides scored with the dusky reds and browns of freshly-turned furrows; the distant woods full of smoky grey shadows.

Fernihirst Castle is now a Youth Hostel. It is an imposing site. The original building dated from 1400: " brent " " throyne downe," in successive assaults, and then finally demolished by order of James VI in 1593. All that was left intact was the cellarage, and upon this was built, in 1598, part of the main block and later the other walls were built up to their present height.

This was the home of that branch of the Kers known as the Fernihirst Kers. There seems no proof that the Kers were of Norman descent. Although there were Kers in the north of England in 1231, and in the counties of Peebles, Ayr and Stirling in 1296 who did homage to Edward I at Berwick, none of these can be claimed with certainty as the ancestors of either Lothian or Roxburghe. The name could be derived from the Celtic " Caer," or fort, but it is of interest to note that the word " ker " in Scotland means left, and the Kers were reputed to be " ker-handed," *i.e.* left-handed.

The descendants of the two families of Ker long continued contentious about the ascendency of one family over the other. In 1590 Robert Ker of Cessford, later first earl, killed William Ker of Ancrum, head of the rival house of Fernihirst. Among the Roxburghe Muniments are preserved the papers relating to the settlement of this feud in 1606.

From the tower I followed a road up the hillside which was the former approach to the castle, and came out on another main road from Jedburgh, high above the Jed Valley overlooking a wide expanse of hill and valley. To the north-west I could see the Eildons in the distance, with Dunion and Ruberslaw nearer at hand, and south to the Cheviots " the road that runs by Carter Bar " to Otterburn. Directly across the valley was Lintalee, a plain grey old house, " modern " only in a comparative sense, which stands within a well-defined medieval earthwork. Here is really the prelude to Otterburn. The good Sir James built his " fair manor " at Jedburgh about 1317 when he was left in charge, along with Sir Walter the Steward, of the kingdom while Bruce was away helping his brother in the Irish wars against Edward I.

Douglas had just finished building and was preparing for his first excursion into Northumberland when one of his spies brought word that an English force was approaching. The story is told in Barbour's *Bruce*. The English had to pass through a thickly wooded pass which, wide enough at first, narrowed sharply, and at this point Douglas laid his ambush. He made a road block of young birch-trees bent down and twisted together, and hid his archers in a recess above with orders not to shoot until his slogan was raised. When the moment came the cry " A Douglas! A Douglas! " sent down a shower of arrows on the first detachment of the English, brought up abruptly against the barrier. A Sir Ros de Richmont, in command, and Douglas met face to face in single combat, and Richmond was slain. The survivors fled with his body, and Arundel decided to abandon the expedition. For this exploit the Douglas had a wreath of stakes, representing the birch trees added to his coat of arms. Thereafter Teviotdale was for long the battleground of the Percy and Douglas families, a Percy at one time receiving Jedburgh Castle from Edward III to whom it had been ceded by Edward Balliol.

At the foot of Swinney Moor, which goes over from Jedburgh, lies Southdean (Chesters), where the Scots army assembled before the battle of Otterburn. The foundations of Souden Kirk where the war council was held are still visible. While exploring that district I stayed at the schoolhouse. It faced south to the same stretch of the Cheviots as I had looked out on from our farm, but now the Border line was but a few miles distant. It was winter then and the mists were often low down. But in high summer I returned again, and while out walking, and following my usual practice of asking directions and information from local people, I stopped to speak to a man at a garden gate. To my surprise and pleasure I discovered he was a cousin of Andrew Lang.

" I was born in this district," he said, " But I went to London University, and now I spend all my vacations here with my family."

I told him I was following the Border line—the easy way.

" I've walked the bit from Deadwater to Rushy Fell many times, and along Carter Fell. It's glorious country, so absolutely desolate. A wonderful change ' for one who has been long in city pent '."

Fired with emulation, I decided to attempt that three-mile stretch from Wauchope Forest, along Carter Fell to Carter Bar. The Forestry Commission's handbook had said this part of the Border line was boggy but passable in dry weather, though " wet at all times."

Two miles of green road led off the main road to the edge of the forest and the ascent to Carter Fell (1,898 feet). On the way I met a shepherd: " See ye dinna lose yerself," he warned. But the day was clear. The climb up was stiffish through heather and bent, but it was only boggy when I struck the line itself, guided there by two cairns to the Ordnance Survey stone. The panorama on both sides of the Border was magnificent, only blurred on the horizon by a heat haze. It was the hottest day of the year, 80° down in Southdean, but up there was a strong cool breeze, which made the gradual ascent to the highest point of the fell easy. I came down at Carter Bar exultant and not at all tired.

I never go over Carter Bar and down to Otterburn without a quickening of the pulse. There was staged that great stainless episode of Border chivalry, " or ever the knightly days were gone."
Scotland and England were then actually at war. Richard II had just led an army over the Border—in 1385—in an attempt to bring the Scots to battle, but the days of Bruce were not too far distant for them to have forgotten his advice that their best defences were the woods and wilds of their hills. Richard got as far as the Firth of Forth, through a scorched land, denuded of supplies, and had to turn back, burning the Abbeys on his way.

It was in retaliation for this raid that the Scots raised, in 1388, an army to invade England. The story goes that an English spy was captured returning from Southdean. He had aroused suspicion by walking instead of riding as a decent Borderer would, and Douglas got details of the English forces and plans. The Scots army was divided in two—the larger section to go through Cumberland, the other, under James, second Earl of Douglas, through Northumberland. The House of Douglas was then at its full glory, rivalled only by the Percies of Northumberland. The two chief protagonists at that period were James, second Earl of Douglas and Henry Percy, the famous Hotspur, eldest son of the third Earl of Northumberland. Both had all the trappings of medieval chivalry—good looks, dashing bearing, gay apparel. Hotspur was twenty-four years of age, Douglas perhaps under thirty.

The English forces were gathered at Alnwick and Newcastle the latter under Hotspur. The Scots under Douglas reached Newcastle, and the French historian, Froissart, states that in a skirmish without the walls Douglas and Percy engaged face to face and Douglas captured the Percy pennon.

" Sir," said Douglas, " I shall bear this token of your prowess into Scotland, and set it on high on my castle of Dalkeith."

" Sir," retorted Percy, " Ye may be sure ye shall not pass the bounds of Northumberland till ye be met withall in such wise that ye shall make none avaunt thereof."

" Well, sir," returned Douglas, " come this night, for I shall plant it before my tent, and see if you can win it back."

After these knightly exchanges Douglas withdrew to await the taking up of his challenge. Nothing happened that night and Douglas retreated further on to Otterburn. Both knights were eager to come to grips, but their military advisers had other views. The English believed the Scots army was immense and that the challenge was a ruse to force a battle. Douglas on the other hand was advised to leave Redesdale at once and link up with the rest of the army at Carlisle. Both disregarded such advice. Douglas filled in the time at Otterburn by besieging the tower there. Hotspur hearing of this set out without waiting for the reinforcements which were coming up under the command of the Bishop of Durham.

And the battle of Otterburn was fought that night of 19 August 1398 under the light of the moon that had lit so many Border raids.

Froissart records that the Douglas was struck down mortally wounded. Sir James Lindsay reached him:

" Cousin, how fares it with you? "

" Indifferently," said the earl... " I count myself dead... Walter and John Sinclair up with my banner and cry ' Douglas,' and let neither friend nor foe know of my state."

The version of the ballad in the *Minstrelsy* has:

> " But I have dreamed a dreary dream
>   Beyond the isle of Skye.
> I saw a dead man win a fight
>   And I think that man was I. . . .
>
> " My wound is deep; I fain would sleep
>   Take thou the vanguard of the three,
> And hide me by the braken bush,
>   That grows on yonder lilye lee.
>
> " O bury me by the braken bush,
>   Beneath the blooming briar.
> Let never living mortal ken,
>   That ere a kindly Scot lies here."

The Scots win the victory and Percy yields gracefully to Sir Hugh Montgomery.

There is an older, and much fuller, version of the ballad of Otterburn (about 1550) in the British Museum (Cotton MS. Cleopatra CIV) than Herd's MS., which was the one used by Scott. There is no mention of the capture of the Percy pennon:

> It fell abought the Lamasse tyde,
>   Whan *ᵃ*husbonds wynnes their haye,   *ᵃ husbandmen*
> The doughtye Douglasse bowynd hym to ryde
>   *ᵇ*In Ynglond to take a praye.   *ᵇ into*

When they reach Newcastle Douglas calls to Percy to " come to the field and fecht," boasting he has burned all Percy's heritage through Bamburghshire, and Percy exclaims:

> ". . . For the trespasse thou hast me done
>   The *ᵃ*tone of us schall dye."   *ᵃ one (of two)*
> " Where schall I *ᵇ*byde thee? " sayd the   *ᵇ await*
>   Dowglas,
>   " Or where wilt thou com to me? "
> " At Otterborne, in the hygh way,
>   There mast thou well logeed be. . . ."
> " There schall I byde thee," says the Dowglas,
>   " By the fayth of my bodye."
> " Thether schall I com," sayd Sir Harry Perssy,
>   " My trowth I plyght to thee."

He hands wine over the walls and bids the Douglas and his men drink.

Later, when he comes up on the Douglas and receives a message from his kin to delay the battle, he scornfully rejects it:

> " My trowth ys plyght to yonne Skottysh
>   knyght,
>   *ᵃ*It nedes me not to *ᵇ*layne . . .   *ᵃ I need not* *ᵇ conceal*
> He wolde me call but a kowarde knyght
>   In hys londe another daye."

They meet in single combat and Percy slays the Douglas, and the ballad has the same conclusion as the Scottish version.

Thys fraye bygan at Otterborne,
Bytwene the nyght and the day;
Ther the Dowglas lost hys lyffe,
And the Perssy was lede awaye.

and the ballad ends with a request to pray for the soul of Percy, " a gentyll knyght."

You will look in vain for the " braken bush," for the Douglas was carried to Melrose Abbey and buried with his ancestors, but there is a cross to mark the battle called, in Northumberland, the Percy Cross.

From Carter Bar the Border line goes over the heights to Whitelaw above Yetholm. Part of it is within the artillery range. Even in Logan Mack's day he did not recommend anyone to do it alone. I followed the metalled road nearest to it that goes by Hounam, and as there is no inn until Morebattle I stayed at a shepherd's cottage while exploring Dere Street.

Imperceptibly the hills grow milder and greener, but the sense of remoteness, of some unbroken antiquity, holds these solitary places along Kale and Oxnam waters.

It was a winter landscape now but I could picture it as a poet saw it:

Oh the sheep herding's lightsome among the green braes
Where Kale wimples clear neath the white blossomed slaes,
Where the wild thyme and meadowsweet scent the soft gale.

" Take the green road up my hill," said the shepherd the first morning, " and you will come out on Dere Street." I found it was well defined between Whitton Edge to Pennymuir. Roman weapons and coins have been found along this stretch. The hill folk would not let the invaders pass unopposed; but Roman camps rose over prehistoric forts, Roman altars were set up beside the stone circles. But this was not to be their Border line—that, the first attempt at a Border line, was to be set farther back at the Wall.

One day I walked nine miles, according to the shepherd's calculation, on Dere Street and other " green roads," ending up in the " green dens of Chatto," beloved of Lady John Scott, who used

H

to wander these Cheviot foothills as she had her native Lammer-muirs before her marriage.

Hounam is a tiny village by the Kale with an ancient church whose patron was, in 1185, John, son of Orm (Ormiston). There is only one tower left standing in the valley between Hounam and Morebattle—Corbet Tower, which is still inhabited.

About here are the famous " singing braes " of Gateshaw—where it is said the praise of the hillside conventicle worshippers in Covenanting days could, by some trick of echo, be heard miles away.

Morebattle village, which has some interesting old houses, and a church mentioned in the *Inquisito Davidis* 1116 stands high and dry now, but its name derives from the older one of Merebotle " the town by the mere." There was once a thousand-acre loch extending towards Yetholm, the last bit being drained in 1832.

I did not stop to explore Morebattle—I was bound for Cessford Castle and Eckford. The castle lies up a side road two miles on from Morebattle. At my first sight of it I thought I had seen nothing more formidable in the Borders. Surrey, who brought up his cannons with some effect against Jedburgh Abbey, failed to break down its walls. They are 12–14 feet thick, and in spite of three great rents from top to bottom looked as if they would stand a few more centuries. From the mound on which it stands I seemed to be looking out through a deep cleft in the hills to the Border line, only seven miles away.

It was the greatest and the last " strength " of the " Cappit Kers," no mere bickerers, but carrying on their feuds on a grand scale until the last of them became the great " pacifier " of the Borders under James VI and I, and it is said to have ended its days as a prison for the Covenanters. Fleurs (Floors Castle) at Kelso became the residence of the Cessford Kers.

Robert Ker of Cessford was the first Lord Roxburghe in 1599 and advanced to Earl of Roxburghe in 1616, when the male line failed, and was continued through a daughter. The fifth Earl was created Duke but the male line again failed when the third Duke died unmarried in 1804. This was the " Literary Duke," who collected the " Roxburghe Manuscripts." The family of Innes Ker, now holds the title.

It will be remembered that in the *Lay of The Last Minstrel*

Scott gives the sorrowful ramifications of the blood feud between the Scotts of Buccleuch and the Kers of Cessford.

In 1552 Walter Scott, then Warden of the Marches, was murdered by the Kers in the High Street of Edinburgh, and it was his widow who was the lady of Branxholme in " The Lay."

Of course these blood feuds were not peculiar to the Borders but were the pattern of medieval times. " Fair Margaret " of Branxholme was but another Juliet with a happier fate.

Among the Roxburghe Papers are preserved two letters addressed to Cessford from Mary Queen of Scots previous to her excursion into the Borders " to see custree (justice) administrat," and later commanding him to co-operate with Lord Hume in consulting with the English Warden, Foster, in sending a force against Liddesdale.

In the whirligig of events a Ker of Fernihirst was to fight on the Queen's side and a Cessford Ker against her.

From Cessford the hills recede and the road runs through the pleasant agricultural land characteristic of the Kelso plain. The towers of Grymsley (Grahamslaw), Eckford, Moss Tower, and Ormiston Castle are remembered only in names of farmlands, yet all have figured in Border history. All were burned in the English raid of 1544, as was also Eckford Church when its bell was carried off to be hung in an English church. The spoils of a fray evidently included church bells. Linton Church bell, it is asserted, was " lifted " from Durham.

There is a well preserved watch tower at Eckford Church gate, reminder of the days of the " resurrectionists." A story of these days was told me by a surviving grandson of the Rev. Joseph Yair who was for over sixty years minister of Eckford. His younger brother was a medical student in Edinburgh, and suspicion had fallen on him. He fled to Eckford Manse and the minister hid him for three months in a roomy cupboard off his study. There were three maids, a sister, the minister's wife and numerous children, in the house, but no one betrayed the refugee. Eventually the minister managed to smuggle his brother out of the house and later out of the country.

Kale enters the Teviot a little way below Eckford Church at lovely Kalemouth House, with its walled garden lying in an angle between the two waters. Lady John Scott's old home, Kirkbank, where now another Border poet, Alexander Buist, lives, neighbours it by but a few yards.

Crailing is close to Eckford and was the chief seat of that clan of Cranston, but there are no Cranstons left in Crailing now.

From Morebattle another road to Kelso skirts the valley of the drained loch and Linton Church stands prominently on a high mound—rather like an ark above the waters. The curiously uniform mound is formed of almost pure sand. A legend tells that it was riddled by two sisters in penance for the sin of a brother in slaying a priest.

Another legend centres on a sculptured stone 800 years old, very much weathered but now protected by glass, above the church porch. It was long thought to be a man on horseback, falcon on shoulder, attacking a wild beast with a spear. This beast, legend says, was the " worm " that lived in a lair by the loch and devastated surrounding crops. It was slain by the Laird of Larriston, who was then a Norman Somerville. He charged the monster with a burning peat on the end of his spear and thrust it down its throat.

But the antiquarians have decided that the monster is but two bears, and that although this Norman tympanum is unique in Scotland it has counterparts in England.

I am always reluctant to spoil a legend. After all, it takes some extraordinary event to create a legend. Strange creatures have emerged and continue to emerge, out of the waters. All this valley of Kale to the Bowmont at Yetholm was once the great Loch of Lynton of medieval records.

From the church I looked down on a knoll in a field which was the site of the tower of these Norman Somervilles. Linton is one of the most beautifully restored parish churches in the Borders thanks to the late minister, the Rev. James Leishman. While the abbeys lay in ruins the parish churches, some of them older than the abbeys, survived through all the vicissitudes of Border history, and in their records there is plenty of drama and human interest. Ecclesiastical history in the Borders, at least, is never dull.

The Rev. James Leishman in his delightful book *Linton Leaves* has fully told the fascinating story of the church and parish.

The Norman font is one of the oldest in Scotland. It is deep enough to allow complete immersion of the babe, but it is alleged that many a Border warrior would contrive to keep the sword-hand of his man-child out of the holy water!

I was most impressed, however, by a memorial to a noted agriculturalist, William Dawson. It suddenly brought into focus an era—that of the transition of this wild reiving country into the rich, peaceful agricultural lands of today. William Dawson was born in the eighteenth century. Scotland, at last able to settle down, began not only to develop but take the lead in the arts of civilisation, astonishing Voltaire into the remark: " at the present time it is from Scotland we receive gifts in taste in all the arts from the epic poem to gardening! "

Thomson produced one of these epic poems, *The Seasons*. His mother had a small estate at Wideopen, a mile or two from the church and Linton claims that she returned to her old home for the birth.

Linton has, however, an undisputed claim to another poet, Thomas Pringle. Coleridge would have elevated him to immortality by declaring his poem " Afar in the Desert " to be among the two or three most perfect lyrics in our language. Perhaps a more enduring claim for greatness lies in the work he did in freeing African slaves.

The road I followed from the church by Linton Burnfoot to Yetholm, is, I think, one of the loveliest in the Cheviot foothills. From where the Kale makes a sudden sweep round Morebattle to Eckford there is no stream until Bowmont Water is reached at Yetholm. But the road follows the bed of the vanished loch, which yet seems to have left a moist greenness on everything. If Wordsworth had come this way instead of by Yarrow he could have written with even greater truth:

> Nor have my eyes by greener hills
> Been soothed in all my wanderings.

IX

Bowmont and Tweed

IT IS NOW over forty years since I first visited Yetholm and fell under its spell. On that first day I bought an ash walking-stick made by a gypsy, and it has been my trusty companion over many miles of the green roads of the Cheviots.

There are really two Yetholms, Town Yetholm, and Kirk Yetholm, separated only by the Bowmont Water. The Bowmont is the only Border stream which rises on the Scottish side and flows through England. Eventually it joins the Till near Wooler. Its source is on the slope of Windygyle in the Cheviots over which the Border line passes. Here was one of the busier " passage ways " and a place of Wardens' meetings. An English Warden, Russell, Foster's son-in-law, was shot at one of these meetings and a prehistoric cairn came to be called " Russell's Cairn."

One day in early December I set out to trace the Bowmont to its source. I was staying at the schoolhouse, and I asked permission to travel so far in the school bus so as to have the most of the daylight for hill walking.

The driver was a Gladstone of the clan " guid at need." His father and grandfather, as the local blacksmiths, had forged the gypsy crown, and his father had crowned the last of the line of Faa. He himself had been about the last of the lads who herded the village cows on the Haugh.

All along the Bowmont (the ancient Bolbent) there is scarcely a farm whose name has not come down from the dawn of history. And aerial surveys have now revealed how thick were the settlements of prehistory.

It was still dark when we left Town Yetholm. Primside, close to the road, was shrouded. These lands had a royal proprietor in Prince Henry, David I's only son. He granted them to the Riddells—one of the oldest surnames in Scotland. Further on I could just discern Attonburn (the old Hattonburn or Aldtonburne

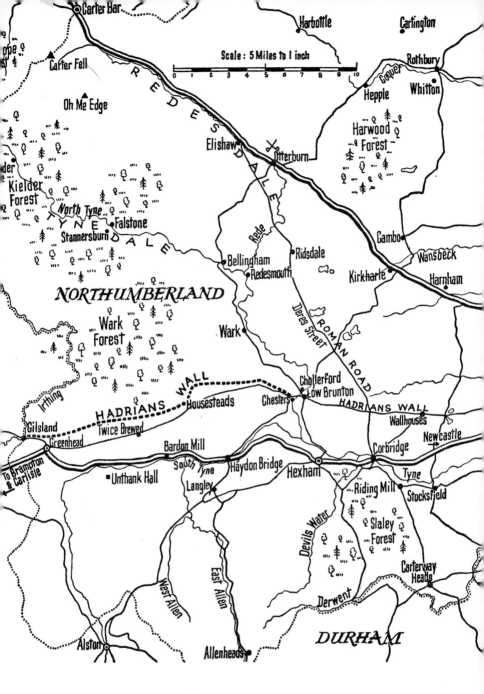

Scale : 5 Miles to 1 inch

0 1 2 3 4 5 6 7 8 9 10

Carter Bar

Harbottle

Carlington

Carter Fell

Rothbury

Coquet

Oh Me Edge

Hepple

Whitton

REDESDALE

Elishaw

Otterburn

Harwood
Forest

Kielder
Forest

North Tyne

Falstone

Stannersburn

TYNEDALE

Rede

Ridsdale

Cambo

Wansbeck

Bellingham

Redesmouth

Kirkharle

Harnham

NORTHUMBERLAND

Wark
Forest

Wark

Deres Street

ROMAN ROAD

Irthing

HADRIANS WALL

Housesteads

Chesters

Chollerford

Low Brunton

HADRIANS WALL

Wallhouses

Gilsland

Twice Brewed

Newcastle

Greenhead

Bardon Mill

Corbridge

To Brampton
& Carlisle

South Tyne

Haydon Bridge

Hexham

Tyne

Unthank Hall

Langley

Riding Mill

Stocksfield

West Allen

East Allen

Devils Water

Slaley
Forest

Carterway
Heads

Alston

Allenheads

Derwent

DURHAM

County of Northumberland

of the charters) across the Bowmont. It is from this fountainhead
of the Cessford Kers that the Roxburghe heir takes his title—the
Marquis of Bowmont.

The haughs spread out here and the old Bolbent seems to have
taken many a " bent," carving new channels, flooding the valley,
but it is now being curbed by strong embankments. The choco-
late-coloured ploughlands looked deep and fertile and the pastures
were still wonderfully green. But in these Cheviot foothills there is
little to mark the change of season. Heather is sparse, there is less
bracken than elsewhere, and the hills remain predominantly green
—turf cropped to their rounded summits.

Just before Belford is the site of Molle, or Mow, church and
burial ground, on a scaur above Bowmont.

Molle was a considerable medieval township, with mills and a
tower, of which nothing now remains. Old Belford House
(seventeenth century) is now the stable, garage and barn of the
pleasant modern farmhouse. A signpost there points up a rough
road: " Hounam 3 miles," but when I walked it another day I
found it soon became a " green road " and petered out completely
beyond a deserted homestead, appropriately called " See Few."

At Cocklawfoot road-end some children got in, and I got off.
Several green roads climb up from about Cocklawfoot Farm by the
Kelsocleuch, Cheviot, and Kingseat burns. I was advised at the
farm that the Kingseat Burn was the one to follow, as the source of
Bowmont.

A grey light had been gradually diffusing itself, but there was
still no sign of sun. The banks of the burn were easy and not at all
boggy. About a mile or so up the glen I sat down on a boulder.
There was an absolute stillness in the air—a hush. Even the sheep
seemed immobile. Suddenly a shaft of sunlight struck an opposite
peak. Without any previous thought, without design, I had
arrived at Cocklawfoot at the supreme moment, as Will Ogilvie
had done:

> When suddenly—back like a slow drawn net
> The mists are drawn up the hillside steep,
>   Till the boulders show, and the white-backed sheep
> Come one by one into open view.
>   Then the heather glints, then a peak breaks through
> Another, another, and each one higher,
>   Till out of the veil leaps a disc of fire,

Floors Castle

PLATE 4
Photograph: The British Travel and Holidays Association

PLATE 5
Jedburgh
Abbey

*Photograph:
The British
Travel and
Holidays
Association*

PLATE 6
Queen
Mary's House

Photograph:
The British
Travel and
Holidays
Association

Branxton: Flodden Memorial in middle distance

PLATE 7
Photograph: The British Travel and Holidays Association

And the sun on the shoulder of Grubbit burns,
And Cheviot wakes and the day returns.

As I followed it, the burn became smaller and smaller, the ground more boggy. Once I stopped to peer into its peaty depth and a sea-trout, startled, leaped into the air and landed at my feet, startling me even more. I helped it back with my stick and continued on until I lost the last trickle in a kind of morass. Up above loomed the Border line.

Again I touched the Border line the easier way—some two miles out of Kirk Yetholm, at Yetholm Mains, where the line leaves the heights for the last time and comes down the Halterburn to Bowmont Water.

The Town Yetholm road crosses the Bowmont and takes a short leap up between the manse and the kirk to the long straggling street of Kirk Yetholm, once a gypsy settlement, which Queen Esther, the last of the royal gypsy queens, said was:

sae mingle-mangle that ye micht think it was
either built on a dark nicht, or sawn [sown] on a windy ane.

Queen Esther Faa Blythe, also pronounced the race's epitaph: " There are nane o' my seed, breed, or generation at Yetholm." When she died in 1883 she was buried with great ceremony, and Lady John Scott, always the gypsies' friend, sent a wreath of white roses.

The gypsies' thatched cottages, including the " Palace," are neatly slated now. Most have been modernised and several bought up by " incomers," for others are discovering the charms of this Cheviot hill village and the vigour of the hill air.

How did these footfree people come to settle in this place? One tradition is that a youth of the Young family (for the gypsies in times of persecution assumed well-known surnames) saved the life of Captain Bennet of Grubbit at Namur: another was that a gypsy recovered a valuable bloodmare stolen from the laird of Marlefield. The latter seems the more likely tale! He built cottages for the gypsy tribe where they could winter, some time about the late seventeenth century, and his successor came to call them his bodyguard. The situation suited the gypsies very well—it was the

" yett " (gate) into England, and the Cheviots a handy smuggling route. Like the reivers, they " lifted " on both sides of the Border, and they had much the same code of loyalty; their word was their bond. Bennet of Marlefield always left his house-key with Will Faa when he left home. But they were feared, for they could be very vengeful.

The Yetholm gypsies were of the Royal Faas, who ruled in Northumberland, Berwickshire and Roxburghshire: the other royal tribe was the Bailyows (or Baillies)—from whom Jane Welsh Carlyle boasted descent—who ruled mostly in the West March from Langholm.

They were styled " Kings and Earls of Little Egypt." Legend clusters thickly round the race. Queen Esther's father claimed Egyptian and Jewish blood and descent from Pharaoh's daughter. Their many words, akin to Hindustani, suggest India as their original country. They seem to have been prominent in Scotland in the reign of James II, but in the time of William the Lion there is mention of " tinklers." " Tinkers " is the name they had in the Borders on account of their trade in tinware. They were in and out of favour with the Stuart monarchs down to the time of Queen Mary. They " dansit before the king " at Holyrood, they were in the train of James IV in Eskdale; and James V, who is said to have written the ballad of the " Gaberlunzie Man," is reputed to have frequented their camps.

As such, the gypsies have a definite place in the pattern of Border history. They were often allies of the reivers too.

How did the gypsy race die out of Yetholm? The Kirk had come to have a great influence over them: they had a great respect for their ministers. They brought their children for baptism and their dead for burial. The Covenanters had bred a race of fearless preachers and it may have been that quality in their ministers that appealed to the gypsies (as it is said to have done to the mosstroopers). In 1829 their minister was the Rev. John Baird, a man of wide culture, co-founder and first President of the Plinian Society in Edinburgh, which had Darwin among its early members. He started a school in Yetholm—said to be the first " ragged school " in Scotland—for the gypsies' children. The gypsies would not give up their own freedom but they let the minister have their children.

The church was a rectory of Kelso Abbey, but its foundation has been lost. Edward I issued state documents from Yetholm, and there is a tradition that many of the slain knights were brought here from Flodden for burial as the nearest consecrated ground in Scotland.

It was on the first spring day in February that I walked the short stretch of some two miles from Kirk Yetholm to the Border line. It was too early to find lambs, but the expectant mothers were in-gathered in the home fields and " turned on to the turnips," as the farming phrase goes. A little beyond the farm cottages the Halterburn crosses under the road and joins the Bowmont. On the far side of the burn a signboard said " England," and into a dyke was built a tablet saying " Northumberland National Park " with the emblem of a whaup.

But I turned back now. The Border line jumps the Bowmont— there are only two places where it *crosses* a river instead of following its course. (The other is at the Whitadder in the Merse.)   It continues up over a ridge on the other side and down into Carham by the Reddenburn into Tweed. It would be difficult to define through these cultivated fields and woods, and there is in fact one part which has apparently never been " settled " and is known as " No-man's-Land." Though I could follow the Mindrum road to Carham, I decided to detour to Kelso and from there cross the Border either at Carham or at Coldstream.

On the bridge over the Bowmont I lingered for a while before taking the other side back to Town Yetholm. The water was big with melted snow from the higher reaches. Looking up at the gentle lines of the hills that enclose this milder part, I went over in thought again all the long tortuous Border line from Scots Dyke, with its no less tortuous history. Here where the Bowmont takes farewell of its Scottish birthplace and becomes an English stream I said my own farewell to the wild hills of the Border line. From now on my way would be through the East March, from the rich agricultural Kelso plains through the " garden of the Merse " to Berwick.

" Kelso," remarked my sister to a London visitor, " was to us the Metropolis." She was referring to the days when we lived on the Lammermuir farm.

Now, some fifty years later, I think the description still fits Kelso. It *is* the farmers' metropolis, a great trading centre, a meeting place for the fraternity, a social centre, a place of education for his children in the modernised High School, and a shopping mecca. You can get almost anything in Kelso from a horseshoe nail to the latest in farm machinery; from oil lamps to the latest electrical equipment; from fresh farm butter to frozen foods. It was a " pretty little market town " in Pennant's day; Scott thought it " the most beautiful if not the most romantic village in Scotland "; and it is a beautiful town today, but still unmistakably an agricultural town.

Kelso suffered as much as any of the Border towns—it is only 4 miles from the Border and on the direct line of march from Northumberland. But Kelso " wears her rue with a difference." It gives you the impression of sunniness—a bright vitality, not a golden languor. The great, sleek Clydesdales have practically disappeared from the farms but Kelso is still a horseloving community. The " Kelsae laddie " during civic week is well mounted and leads the riders to Yetholm. Horse-jumping figures largely at St James's Fair—now the largest agricultural show in the south of Scotland, and which is Kelso's big day.

A respect of letters, and especially of poetry, has always been a feature of Scottish rural life, and it seems fitting that it was in Kelso that, in his aunt's garden, sloping pleasantly to Tweed, Scott first read Percy's *Reliques of Ancient Poetry*. He has recorded the excitement of that moment—an excitement that never really left him all his life: " The summer day sped onward. . . . I forgot the hour of dinner, was sought with anxiety and still found entranced." When we lose that sense of excitement we shall be poor indeed.

Scott, who got most of his early schooling in Kelso Grammar School, would inhale a literary atmosphere from the start. He found in Kelso " a respectable subscription library, a circulating library of ancient standing and some private bookshelves " into which he " waded like a blind man into a ford." Kelso was already ancient in literature before the monks came—it was the Calchvynyd mentioned by Taliessen, the sixth-century bard, a name that means chalk hill and which survives in the " chalk-heugh " of the north bank of Tweed. The fifteenth-century monks, Brother James and Prior James, were celebrated scribes— the latter translated a Latin " Rural Affairs " into Scots verse.

It was inevitable that here Scott should, at the age of thirteen first feel " the awaking of that delightful feeling for the beauties of natural objects " combined with " the historical incidents, or traditional legends connected with many of them ... which at times made my heart feel too big for its bosom."

This is the recurring theme of all Border literature, which no writer on the Borders in all sincerity can neglect.

The Chalkheugh is walled and terraced now since the great flood of 1810 which threatened to undermine it. Rennie's bridge of 1803, on which he tried his prentice hand before he took it as a model for London's Waterloo Bridge, still throws its five graceful arches over the united waters of Teviot and Tweed.

I love to stand on Maxwellheugh, over the bridge, on a summer day when the sunlight turns the buff-coloured town to a pale amber, and the waters, spread out to a lagoon-like expanse, mirror the walls of Chalkheugh, and swans float lazily as swans have done from time out of mind: or when the sun goes down in a frosty winter sky and the tides run crimson under the bridge, and see how the town holds at its heart its dusky ruin.

The fields round Kelso are golden on an autumn day of harvest. Do the reapers remember?

> They smile and pass, the children of the sword,
>   No more the sword they wield,
> And, o, how deep the corn
>   Along the battle field.

Stevenson should have been writing of Kelso.

That Yetholm February day's hint of spring was maintained, and now in mid-February I took the road again.

The Coldstream road, which leaves the Market Square, keeps close to the level haughs of Tweed and merges insensibly into the Merse, the other great agricultural region of the Borders. The Carham–Cornhill road leaves Maxwellheugh, and is further away from the river and nearer the Cheviot foothills. Beyond Carham towards Wark the transition is sharper—the land has a darker tone, the Northumbrian Cheviot hills loom up in the distance.

Before reaching Carham the valley opens out and there is a wide view to the Lammermuirs with Hume Castle standing out in the foreground with a watchful eye to the English Border. You

realise how it came to be called " the Watchdog of the Merse,"
and how easily it could pick up the warning beacons from Northumberland in the time of the threatened French invasion.

It was the headquarters of the hereditary Wardens of the East
March, the Homes. But of the origins of that family I have already
written in my previous book. As Wardens they would meet with
the English Wardens at Haddonshank and Reddenbank.

The Reddenburn, reached about one mile before Carham, was
the Border line and the beginning of the East March. It is an
insignificant, almost ditchlike, water which can be easily jumped.

I found a gate and followed it to where the burn falls into
Tweed. Here again for the last time I stood where the two coun-
tries and three counties meet—Roxburghshire, Berwickshire, and
Northumberland.

From here the Border line follows the bed of Tweed as in Esk and
Liddel. At this end of the line, the usual wrangling took place
over the settlement of the boundary. To quote from the old
Perambulation of the Borders (1222).

> Hugh de Bolebec to the King: ... on the quinzaie Michaelmas,
> being the day fixed by the King of Scotland, he with the knightes of
> Northumberland met in person at Revedeburne David de Lyndesay,
> Justiciar of Lothian, Patrick Earl of Dunbar and many other knights
> sent by the King of Scotland ... they elected six knights for Eng-
> land and six for Scotland. ... Whereon the six English knights
> with one assent proceeded by the right and ancient Marche between
> the kingdoms, the Scottish knights totally dissenting and contradict-
> ing them. ...

Twelve more knights were called in, six on either side " for
greater security," but the record continues:

> The English knights agreed on the said boundaries, and the Scottish
> knights to different ones as before. And inasmuch as the Scottish
> knights thus stood in the way of the business, the writer, in virtue of
> the King's command, elected and caused to be sworn twentyfour
> discreet and loyal knights of his county, that they might settle the
> ancient marches. ...

The English knights then declared what these Marches were but the foresaid justiciar and earl with their knights, resisting with violence hindered them by threats from so doing.

One can imagine the scene.

But the Border line here remains today much as Bolebec described it to his king. It descends from the Cheviots above Yetholm, instead of continuing along their crest to Wooler. Had it done so the whole of Tweed and its tributaries, College Water and Bowmont, would be in Scotland.

Malcolm II won the battle of Carham, 1018, which gave the Lothians, previously in Northumbria, to Scotland. The battle was fought nearer to Wark than Carham, but today Carham station is in Scotland, and Carham village is in England. The village with its parish church, row of well-kept manorial cottages and Hall, is almost dramatically English. So is the very straight long road, lined with avenue trees of immense girth, leading from the village. Except for the bit that rises to the " Kaim " (meaning a ridge in the form of a cockscomb) I had not walked such a level stretch for a long time.

Wark Castle is the English " watchdog " of the East March. It was to the English what Jedburgh and Roxburgh were to the Scots —and has much the same history. Immediately above Tweed and close to a ford, it was a base for invasion from both sides— according to whichever country was in possession.

> Auld Wark upon the Tweed
> Has mony a man's deid.

is a Northumberland saying.

Wark has its version of the romantic story of the founding of the Order of the Garter. The Scots had raided Alnwick and on their way back besieged Wark. In the dark of night Sir William Montague slipped out of the castle and got away and contacted Edward III at Newcastle, who advanced. The Scots retreated and the King entered the castle with great fanfare, and held a ball to celebrate, dancing with the Countess of Salisbury, which led to the famous incident.

Beyond Wark, Tweed takes another of its wide sweeps. And here the eccentric Border line shows one of its strangest quirks. From the bed of the Tweed it ascends to English ground, encloses a half moon of haugh for about half a mile and then returns to the water! This piece of ground appears in old maps as Scotch Haugh.

The light was now beginning to go rapidly. I was hurrying to catch the 6 p.m. bus for Kelso at Cornhill. The lights of Coldstream were already twinkling across the Tweed and the Hirsel woods showed darkly. The Hirsel is the residence of the Earls of Home, and its beautiful woods are open annually to the public when the rhododendrons are in full glory. In these woods Major Henry Douglas Home, younger brother of the present Earl, and the B.B.C.'s popular " Birdman," has made many bird broadcasts. I thought of one tonight—two blackbirds, on opposite sides of the Border line, singing to each other in harmony across the Tweed.

X

The East March

COLDSTREAM, without appearing to have any noticeably ancient buildings, is one of these places that gives the impression of age. As the only town directly on the Border line between Gretna and Berwick, and with a famous ford that has been crossed by almost every invading army, from whichever side, it recalls much history.

From the bridge over the Leet where it joins Tweed the long rising High Street is most attractive, and has some characteristic Anglo-Scottish houses, but I had to turn down an alley to find the older houses in the Market Square. Some have been restored in character. A tablet on one of the restored buildings marks the "Headquarters of the Coldstream Guards 1659." General Monk seems to have merged two corps into one at Coldstream. The men were chiefly Borderers from both sides. After some years of campaigning he took the regiment to London and it became later the famous Coldstream Guards.

In an angle of the ground where Leet joins Tweed was a priory of Cistercian nuns, dating to the twelfth century, but it has now disappeared. In what was probably the garden a great quantity of human bones was unearthed. Tradition says that the Prioress sent out vehicles to Flodden to bring back the more illustrious dead. Yetholm, Branxton, and Coldstream graveyards were not big enough to hold the dead of Flodden.

From the square I followed the "Nuns Walk"—where Tweed comes close up to the walls—to the fine eighteenth-century bridge.

The Old Toll House on the Scottish side was almost as popular as Gretna for runaway marriages. I did not cross the bridge that day, but instead took the road to Birgham which is about a couple of miles on the way to Kelso. It is almost directly opposite the Border line at Reddenburn. You could pass Birgham as a small and insignificant village, but an event that took place there was momentous—the signing of a treaty that was to ensure " the peace and tranquility of both kingdoms, and that mutual affection should continue between their peoples for all time." For all time! There was to be instead over three centuries of strife.

Scotland had just suffered a numbing blow. In 1286 Alexander III died, and the Golden Age of the Borders, of its abbeys and scholasticism and peaceful husbandry was at an end. An anonymous poet wrote:

> Quhen Alysandyr our king was ^adede,   *a dead*
> That Scotland led in luv and ^ble,   *b law*
> Away was ^csons of ale and brede,   *c plenty*
> Of wine and wax, of gamyn and gle;
> Our gold was changit into ^dlede.   *d lead*
> Christ, born into virginitie,
> Succour Scotland and remede,
> That ^estad is in perplexitie.   *e beset*

The only heir, the Maid of Norway, Alexander's granddaughter, was to be brought back to Scotland " free and quit of all contract of marriage," a promise solemnly affirmed by both Scots and English in the Treaty of Salisbury on 6 November 1289. But Edward I had secretly applied to the Pope for a special dispensation for the marriage of Margaret, the Maid, to his son, which passed the papal seals on 16 November 1289, and the Scots raised no objection to Edward I's proposal. A new treaty of marriage was prepared and completed at Birgham, in July 1290, in which Scottish sovereignty was guaranteed.

Edward I was a great monarch—for England. As was Elizabeth, but they both lamentably failed to understand the Scots. A modern local historian—the late Howard Pease of Otterburn Tower, Northumberland, comments:

> It was thereafter that he [Edward] failed as a statesman. From this failure sprang the " Deadly Feud " between England and Scotland, in which Northumberland bore the brunt. . . . His wise policy to unite England and Scotland by marriage of his son with the heiress of Scotland had been frustrated by the death of the Maid. . . . After that sad happening he determined to achieve union by force of arms and thus sowed the dragon's teeth . . . the Northumberland border was soon to be the " daungerest place in England."

My way now was to be on through the East March to Ladykirk and Norham, separated only by a bridge over Tweed. It was through quiet unexciting farmland with sturdy farmhouses and cottages, and small fields between hedges whose neat scheme of things was only broken by light woodlands. These are the good lands of the Merse, which had been the best ruled of the three Marches.

On entering the parish of old Upsettlington, which includes Ladykirk, the main roads begin to come up from England by Norham and Tweedmouth, and old toll houses still mark the route. This was a great smuggling country, by coast and road, and Simprim farm barns were a useful cache.

Graden is the home of the Milne Homes, who claim descent from the " fighting parson," John Todd, whom Lady John Scott celebrates in one popular song. The family also had a sporting parson, the Rev. George Home. He would set off on Sunday evening, if the meet was on a Monday, with a red hunting coat under his clerical black.

The daffodils were coming out on the long drive of Ladykirk House, and lambing had started in the fields around Old Ladykirk farm. The fairs used to be held in a field in front of the farmhouse. This field, still called Fairfield, falls sharply to Tweed and has one of the best views of Norham Castle. Indeed it was in the next field, the Minister's Glebe, that Scott and Turner viewed the castle, and Turner, from a little lower down, painted his picture.

Scott's Marmion was a fictitious character, but there was a real Marmion who came to the " daungerest place in England " to break a lance for his Lady.

As I looked out across the strip of bright water that is Tweed to those tremendous walls of Norham Castle I felt that there was symbolised all the might and opposition of England. Down below, where Tweed makes another of its wide sweeps, the line, keeping to midstream, leaves one island in England and one in Scotland. There at Norham Edward received the claimants to the Scottish throne. The first step was being taken. Flodden Field lay on the distant horizon.

They would come, these great barons—many of them still with more Norman than Scots blood in their veins—in their magnificent medieval array, vassals of Edward for lands still held in England, willing as such to swear allegiance (with reservations) in the hope of gaining the crown of Scotland. The Bruces of Annandale were there, soon to become more Scottish than Norman, more fiercely allied to their Scottish lands, and to write some of the most glorious chapters in early Scottish history; and the Balliols, to provide Scotland's puppet kings for a season and go down in ignominy. But even then, behind all the ambition of these nobles, the intrigue, the Scottish Commons stood out. They would have none of Edward, and when he gave them John Balliol they called him contemptuously " the toom tabard " (empty coat). With their king " thirled " to Edward they had lost their independence, but they only waited for a Wallace to lead them. It was always a man and not a king to whom they rallied.

> A! fredome is a nobil thing!
> Fredome *a*mayss man to haiff liking.   *a* makes
> Fredome all solace to man giffis.
> He *a*levys at *b*ess that frely levys!   *a* lives *b* ease
> (Barbour, *c.* 1320–1395)

But Edward at first went slowly; the decision was not made at Norham at that first meeting, but more than a year later. He firmly believed in his own role as a great lawmaker—already so successful with his own people and later with the Welsh.

" I will build a church that neither fire nor water can destroy," James IV had declared, when, after he had escaped drowning in the salmon steill, or deep pool, opposite Norham, in gratitude he vowed to dedicate a church to the Virgin Mary. So Ladykirk, or Church of the Steil, was built of nothing but local stone without a particle of wood in its fabric. It stands today as it was built, except for the addition of wooden doors, and wood pews which replaced the stone seats in the last century, and modern stained glass windows in place of the ancient glass. Glass in James IV's time was a rarity and accounted for £67 of a quoted figure of £1,200 for the complete structure.

This pre-Reformation church looks as austere as any Covenanter's kirk. Its beauty is entirely in its stonework within and without, and the style of architecture, which is stated to be " late pointed Gothic," showing the strong French influence of the then dominant " Auld Alliance," yet, like the pele towers which owed their origin to the Normans, with an evolved Scottish style quite its own.

After the beginning of the building in 1500 James IV often visited the church. Records show that he attended services there in 1501, 1505, and 1507 while yet it would be uncompleted. He made rich gifts of embroidered cloths and commended his quarriers for their work, giving them special " drink silver."

Within the church there is preserved an interesting wooden kist elaborately carved, presented by the late Lady Marjoribanks. This is an old alms chest, probable date 1651, originally in St Nicolas's Church, Liverpool. At times they have raised the question of its return but it has been in Ladykirk since 1885.

On the wall behind is a small shield with the Robertson crest, and the crude figure of a ruffianish-looking man. This is the " wild man in chains." A Robertson of Struan captured one of the murderers of James I.

The Robertsons became lairds of Ladykirk in 1737. Before that the barons of the old ville of Hupsettlington and ville of Twedmere went back to 1212-37. Several times the Robertson line has passed to the female heir, her husband taking the name of Robertson. Today the Laird is Major Askew, who has not taken the name of Robertson.

The monks of Ladykirk were much exposed to raids from the English, and they would often see fires alight on both sides. In 1394 the priest of Ladykirk complained that his parish brought him little or nothing as it was so close to the English East March, and leases of land hereabout always had a clause inserted for remission of rent when the land was " herrit " by the " auld enemy." A record stating that Bothwell, as Warden, decided 1000 complaints from the English within Ladykirk's walls, gives a hint of what a Border frontier church was like in these days.

As I was leaving, I stopped and looked round the bare stone church again. It would be alive with colour and movement and the sound of music when James IV came with his court. Did he pay a last visit with his knights to the now completed church on the eve of Flodden? His guns had been mounted in the Fairfield and Norham had surrendered. Was he in high spirits, knowing that no other Scottish king had led a larger and better-equipped army against England? He would revive the old spirit of chivalry—challenges given and taken, the hand-to-hand single combat, and then—freedom for the great Crusade. His Queen had begged him with tears not to go, reminding him " that sche had bot ane sone in to him, quhilk was ane waek warand to the realme of Scotland, and owre soune to him to pase to battell livand so small successioun behind him "—but was she not Harry's sister? And another Queen had called him her " lufe " showing him that " sche had sufferit mekill rebuke for his saik in France for defending of his honour, scho beleiffit suirlie that he wald recompence her againe witht sum of his knyghtlie support in her necessatie, that he wald raise hir armie and cum three fute on Inglis ground for her sake; to that effect scho send him ane ring of hir finger with XI117 thowsand frinche crouns to make his expenses." He had not been too happy about the sudden apparition at Linlithgow during his devotions: " Schir king, my mother hes send me to the desiring the nocht to pass at this tyme . . . ffor gif thow goes thow wilt nocht fair weill in thy journay . . . forther scho bad the nocht mell witht no wemen, nor witht thair counsall," but no doubt it was some man dressed up as St James to frighten and dissuade him.

But perhaps he came into the church, to kneel, humbly and alone, fingering the iron chain girdle he had worn, adding a link each year, in penance for his youthful part in the rebellion which ended in the murder of his father. On some sudden impulse did he take it off then in the kirk of Our Lady and give it into the keeping of some priest?

The road from Ladykirk to where the Border line comes to land again beyond Paxton, which I followed a few weeks later, was one of the quietest I have taken even in that quiet Merse farmland. The Tweed is soon out of sight, the fields lie level and uneventful to the eye, but the mind responds to its ancient history. Old place names speak of Anglo-Saxon times when King Edgar gave the Horndean lands to Coldingham Priory, and the Abbot came to fish, for salmon, in his Manor of Fishwick; and the " drengs " of Horndean tilled their land under a feudal law peculiar to Northumberland, which gave them a status above the bondmen sold with the land.

This land had always been richly pastoral, along with the lower reaches of Teviot. Hertford was surprised into recording:

> We would little have thought to find so fair a country in Scotland as the Merse and Teviotdale, nor so plentiful in corn as we found it.

Along this road came, in 1294, the enraged Edward I to the sack of Berwick, the invasion of Scotland, the dethroning of his puppet king (goaded at last by repeated humiliations and taunts of his people into an alliance with France against England); the removal to Westminster of the ancient Stone of Destiny on which the Scottish kings were crowned, and the taking of the Holy Rood of St Margaret, thus striking at the very heart of the Scottish Throne and Church.

He had crossed the ford at Coldstream, spent the night in the Priory, was joined by Anthony Bek of Norham Castle at Ladykirk, reached Hutton that evening and arrived at Nunslees to circle the town by Halidon Hill.

Leaving Edward's route at Paxton village I pressed on to Paxton Old Toll House which marks the Berwickshire boundary and the beginning of Berwick bounds. These bounds are still ridden in conjunction with the great May Day Fair. As Berwick is technically in England this is one Common Riding that should be conceded to England. The Common Riding commenced in the seventeenth century, and the fair booths are still set up in the High Street.

About half a mile from Paxton I came out on a busy highway again—the Berwick–Kelso main road, along which had wound the long caravans from the monasteries bearing wool to Berwick, where the Flemish merchants would receive it in their Red Hall in the Woolmarket for export to Flanders. There were even good roads in the Borders in these days—this road alone reached to Lesmahagow. Berwick, the old Lanercost Chronicle says, was " A second Alexandria whose riches were the sea and its walls the water." It is a strange anomaly that an English town should still give its name to a Scottish county.

At the county noticeboard I turned down a lane to Tweed. It was very broad and rather dull between flattish banks. A fisherman pointed out where the Border line leaves the water midstream and crosses the Berwick–Kelso road.

The line then continues up the farm entry of Ganeslaw, passes beyond and crosses the Whitadder at right angles—the second time the line crosses a river—to Edrington and Mordington, traverses Halidon Hill to Lamberton Toll and plunges over a steep cliff into the sea, leaving a large slice of Scotland, north of Tweed, and its ancient port in England.

I did not propose to explore it any further, but to follow Tweed to Berwick and then cross into Northumberland to pick up the threads of the Flodden story. The day was fine and dry and there was already a salty tang in the air which made my last four miles of walking on the Scottish side of the Border line very stimulating.

On the crest of the road that climbed to join the Duns road by Halidon Hill I looked down on old Berwick town with its Flemish red-pantiled roofs and bridges to Tweedmouth.

Hereabouts Edward I would pause and survey the town. He was probably near enough to hear the shouted taunts of the citizens: " Kyng Edward, wanne thou havest Berwic, pyke thee; wanne thou havest getten, dyke thee " (when you have won Berwick it will be soon enough to wall it).

If Edward had any thought of clemency it vanished then. He leaped the ditch which was the only defence, on his great horse Bayard, and personally directed the terrible slaughter that has gone down in history as " the sack of Berwick."

" ' Knight without reproach ' as he was, he looked calmly on at the massacre of the burghers, and saw in William Wallace nothing but a common robber," writes Green, the English historian.

The Flemings held out in their Red Hall till the last of them, it is said, perished in the burning building. The English fleet had sailed up the Tweed on a favourable tide but were met by citizens, including women, bearing burning brands to set fire to the ships and were unable to land and had to retreat with the tide.

For a day and a half, the Lanercost Chronicle records, the terrible massacre went on. At last a procession of priests bearing the Host reached Edward and begged for mercy. Edward, with one of those sudden revulsions of feeling for which he was well known, ordered the slaughter to cease, and put 400 men to burying the dead.

Trevelyan comments:

What then had Scotland gained by resisting England?—Nothing at all, except her soul, and whatsoever things might come in the end from preserving that.

It was to take Scotland three more centuries of wars to maintain her independence and almost another century to recover from these wars.

Edward stayed long enough in Berwick to start the fortifications, part of the foundations of which can still be seen, though the present walls are Elizabethan. Then he left to subdue the country north of Tweed. Returning in August 1296, he set up a little Parliament and Exchequer modelled on that of England, and, satisfied that Scotland was conquered, returned to England.

But Scotland was not finished. In revenge for the sack of Berwick the Scots raided into Tynedale savagely. Wallace, who won the battle of Stirling Bridge, was back in Berwick with his Scots. In 1305 he was betrayed, it is said, and captured by Sir John Menteith, taken to London, and condemned as a traitor—to a king he had never acknowledged. Part of his body was sent to Berwick to be exhibited as an example to the people.

Still Scotland was not finished. Bruce and Bannockburn were to follow.

But Berwick never recovered from that first terrible blow. It had no chance to do so in all these long years of Border warfare. It was the key to Scotland, and changed hands many times before it was finally lost to England.

Berwick had seen the beginning of the War of Independence and the rise of the mosstrooper, and Berwick saw the end.

In the closing years of Elizabeth's reign Scott of Buccleuch and Ker of Cessford, voluntarily gave themselves up. Sir Robert Carey was then deputy to his father Hunsdon, Warden of the English East March, and in his *Memoirs* he describes the closing scenes

> There had been commissioners in Barwicke chosen by the queene [of England] and the king of Scottes, for the better quieting of the Borders. . . . The English officers did punctually, at the day of peace deliver their prisoners, and so did most of the officers of Scotland; only the lord of Bocleuch and Sir Robert Kerr were faultie. They were complained of and new days appointed. Bocleuch was the first that should deliver. . . . He chose for his guardian Sir William Selby, Master of the Ordinance at Barwicke. . . . Sir Robert Kerr (contrary to all men's expectation) chose mee for his guardian, and home I brought him to my own house. I lodged him as well as I could and tooke order for his diet and men to attend on him . . . and sent him word that (although his harsh carriage towards mee ever since I had that charge, he could not expect any favour yet) hearing so much goodness of him, that hee never broke his word, if should give mee his hand and credit to be a true prisoner, he would have no guard sett

upon him and have free liberty for his friends in Scotland to have ingresse and regresse to him as oft as he pleased. He tooke this very kindly at my handes, accepted of my offer and sent mee thanks.

A little later Ker sent for Carey and they " had it out " or as Carey puts it,

> after long discourse charging and recharging one another . . . at last before our parting wee became good friends . . . hee kept his chamber no longer, but dined and supt with mee. I took him abroad with mee at least thrice a weeke a hunting, and every day we grew better friends.

Ker promised that on regaining his liberty he would not forget, and Carey concludes:

> After his retourne home I found him as good as his word. Wee mett oft at days of truce and had as good justice as I could desire; and so wee continued very kinde and good friends all the time I stayed on the March.

The end was in sight now. On 7 April 1603, James VI arrived in Berwick as king of the United Kingdom, with a large retinue of Scots and English and was received at the boundary. Two days later he crossed Tweed to his new kingdom, knighting Sir Ralph Grey at the bridge.

XI

The Brave of Both Nations

CROSSED THE BRIDGE at Berwick in the Cornhill bus. We passed
the side road to Norham and other roads to Ford and Etal—
two of the loveliest villages in Northumberland. Already the
shadow of Flodden lies on the land "Sum says," Pitscottie re-
marks, " he forgot the warning ' to mell with no wemen '." But
the known facts do not bear out the slander of the love intrigue
with Lady Heron at Ford.

I got out at Twizel Bridge, the narrow old stone bridge that
spans Till under the ruins of Twizel Castle. Till comes down from
the Wooler plain through the wooded parklands of Tillmouth
House—so slowly that the grey-green waters scarcely seem to
move. I could imagine how the contrast between Till at this
point with the temperamental swift-rising Tweed it is so soon to
join, would impress itself on country thought. But notice how the
beat of the lines is like the slow lapping of water:

> Said Tweed tae Till
> What *a*gars ye *b*rin sae still?   *a makes* *b run*
> Said Till tae Tweed,
> Though ye rin wi' speed
> And I rin slaw,
> Where ye droun ae man
> I droun twa.

Only below the steep scaur on which Twizel Castle stands is the
surface broken. There an outcrop of rock forms a small linn.

This was the fateful bridge the English advance-guard crossed to
come between James IV and his retreat into Scotland.

It is generally agreed by both the old chroniclers and later
historians that James saw the English army gather on Wooler
Haugh and later draw off in the direction of Berwick. What

happened after that is a matter of controversy. The old accounts that he would not attack while the enemy was exposed on the bridge can be discredited in face of other facts. The manoeuvre could not be seen from Flodden, and he may have been ill-served by his scouts.

Challenges had been given and taken. Surrey had said he would meet him not later than Friday, 9 September. It was, as R. L. Mackie puts it in his *James IV*, perhaps the best historical account, " an appeal from the General to the knight-errant." James had agreed to wait until mid-day.

Again accounts of what transpired vary. As Mackie says there is a lack of contemporary accounts on the Scottish side: " The Scots who escaped wanted only to forget: no account of the battle by a Scottish soldier is known to exist."

As Child says, the battle of Flodden called out a great deal of verse: he quotes two ballads, refers to some " forgeries," and the one edited by Weber as " inferior."

At Wooler I was shown a long ballad purporting to be written about the time of Elizabeth, and edited with notes by Robert Lambe, Vicar of Norham-on-Tweed, 30 January 1773, but which Weber rejects.

Whether spurious or not, I found it interesting as giving the list of the great English families and Border clans represented in the battle: Percy, Neville, Grey, Dacre, Stanley coming in for special mention. It is an equivalent to the roll call of the Scottish clans in the " Raid of the Reidswire." (But Dacre's English Borderers were to give him more trouble than help.)

The ballad follows accepted tradition: Surrey's movement to Barmoor and King James being advised to retreat to Scotland and refusing: the Scots movement in haste to Branxton Hill, burning the camp litter behind them: the two armies suddenly finding themselves face to face, " not past a quarter mile " as the smoke clears. The valour of the Scots is stressed. Some controversial points get support; Heron comes to Howard's aid: David Home is killed: the English soldiers, like the Scots, cast off their shoes to get a grip of the slippery hillside: the Scots captains and the King's standard bearer " failed at his feet."

That picture of the " unbroken ring " round the King as described by Scott has been questioned:

> The stubborn spearmen still made good
> Their dark impenetrable wood,
>   Each stepping where his comrade stood
> The instant that he fell.
> No thought was there of dastard flight;
> Linked in the serried phalanx tight,
> Groom fought like noble, squire like knight. . . .

But even if James was in the forefront of the battle seeking a hand-to-hand encounter with the English leader, as seems likely with one of his impetuous nature, he would not be deserted by his knights. They would not be a step behind him as he fell wounded —within a spear's length of Surrey, as Surrey testified.

" The Scots love me worst of any Inglishman," said Dacre, " be reason that I fand the body of the King of Scots."

With James fell, according to English statistics, ten thousand of his subjects, including the young archbishop of St Andrews (his natural son), at least two bishops and two abbots, eleven earls and fifteen lords. Burgesses, Mosstroopers and Highlanders were there.

Lord Home, with his men of the Merse, led the only successful assault, and escaped. Pitscottie says that he replied to Huntly, pleading for a second attack: " He dois weill that dois for himself. Lat the laif do thair pairt as we."—a remark completely out of character with the records of the " fiery Homes."

That the Mersemen considered that a victory had been won and started to plunder is quite possible. Plunder was the recognised pay of the medieval soldier. By feudal law they were bound to follow their lords, and find their own supplies.

But it is assumed that the Mersemen went no further than Cold-stream with their booty, as Home and his men appeared on the battlefield the next morning and made an attempt to save the guns. They were beaten back by Howard. This does not look like desertion.

A family historian, the late Major Logan Home, writing of Sir David Home of Wedderburn, who had eight sons, seven of whom were known as " the seven spears of Wedderburn," states:

> They all fought at Flodden, where Lord Home commanded the left wing of the Scottish army and routed the English opposed to him, chasing them off the field of battle—an error which led to the English army gaining an advantage. Sir David tried to persuade his

chief to return from the pursuit of the English, but failing to do so he
and his followers returned and he and his eldest son were killed.

The defeated and bitter remnant of the Borderers were perhaps
too ready to believe the slander and out of it grew the old song,
" The Souters o' Selkirk ":

Up wi' the souters o' Selkirk
And doun wi' the Earl of Home!

But the story is told that on the night of the " False Alarm,"
when the disappointed volunteers gathered at Dalkeith, the Earl
of Home, with nice sense of timing or that irrepressible humour of
the Borderer, requested the Selkirk contingent to enliven the
company by singing " Up wi' the Souters o' Selkirk." They
declined, so he sang it himself, and was enthusiastically acclaimed
as one of themselves.

I had never been to Flodden, until in 1961 the late Sir John
McEwen took me over the field. But, first, he suggested that my
niece and I should go to Marchmont and see the " Flodden flag "
which is presumed to have been carried at Flodden, " the style of
lettering dating it to that period." The flag would probably be kept
at Hume Castle, which was purchased in 1750 by the third Earl of
Marchmont. In 1961 Marchmont was the home of Sir John
McEwen, a president of the Saltire Society and a distinguished
poet.

The flag is now very frail but has been beautifully mounted
between two sheets of glass. In shape a pennon, it shows the
Saltire Lion passant, motto " Keyp Reull " and a parrot or popinjay. No other flag has this motto (and it is not the Home motto)
which points to it being made specially for a Warden. The
Homes had three popinjays on their shield, commemorating an
heiress Nicola Pepdie of Dunglass. Though other families have
the popinjay this one is collared, which is unusual in Scottish
heraldry.

From Marchmont we went straight to Flodden Field crossing by
Coldstream Bridge. In a field to the left of the road is the tradi-
tional " King's Stone " where King James is said to have fallen.
It is of course a prehistoric stone. The Scots army had, however,

straddled what is now the Wooler road. James had marched more than his " three fute of ground into England."

We followed the second signpost to Flodden and Branxton, which passes Encampment Farm. Flodden Edge rose above it to the south-west. Here at Encampment, Sir John McEwen thinks, the army was encamped, where there was water, and only the scouts on the ridge, where there was none. From the ridge they could see the English army encamped at Barmoor. They saw them move off but could not see Twizel Bridge owing to the undulations of the land.

Then Sir John McEwen, who has made a deep study of the battle, took us from point to point, pausing to describe the various positions, and probable movements as he understood them: here were the Highlanders under Lennox and Argyll; there the burgesses under Crawford and Montrose; the men of the Merse under Huntly and Home. The main body was commanded by the King and the flower of his knights.

" What do you think of the vexed question of the men of the Merse under Home? " I asked.

" The left wing division under Home," he said, " came up against Howard and routed him, chasing him off the field. Howard's contingent had the baggage in the rear and no doubt the Mersemen stopped to pillage it and went off to Coldstream with what they could carry. On the other hand Fletcher, the Selkirk survivor, was with the burgess division which was defeated and it may have been that he carried the story to Selkirk. This is only surmise of course."

We seemed to move over a living map, and as Sir John told the story of the battle it seemed to pass inexorably to its final disaster. Again and again he would pause on some inexplicable incident or sudden decision: " Why, why? . . . No man knows."

" One man, and one man only," he said at one point, " seems to have divined Surrey's strategy—old Angus—and he warned the King and advised retreat to Scotland before he was cut off. But the King scorned his warning: ' If you are afraid,' he said, ' Go home.' Angus went, but left his son who was killed beside the King."

" Why," I asked, " was the King not wearing the iron chain when his dead body was found? "

" He was ' fey.' He had worn it as a penance in life. Now he was going to die."

Do we Scots make too much of Flodden? I asked myself.
Scotland was, and still is, sparsely populated compared to the
south. James IV took the very prime of Scottish men with him to
Flodden and the toll was unprecedented. The tragedy was that
Scotland had seemed, in his reign, to be slowly working up to another Golden Age. I thought of Sir John McEwen's own beautiful " Ballad of Flodden ":

> Fallen the Crown—
> such woes betide—
> and stricken down
> our royal pride
> and within the high walls of Linlithgow shall howlets abide.

Surrey with his exhausted and starving army—his camp had
been looted by the English Borderers—moved south. No need to
secure the country. The Scots had no leaders left.

We climbed to the memorial on the hill of Branxton, with its
simple inscription, void of any proportioning of blame, where each
year at the Coldstream festival riders from both sides of the Border
meet to pay tribute " to the brave of both nations."

The fairness of the prospect catches at the throat. All around is
spread the lovely lowlands of both countries, caught between the
Lammermuirs and the Cheviots. Only one small bend of Tweed,
glittering in the sun spoke of any boundary line.

Flodden Field seemed so small in that expanse.

> Noble the shield
> that broken lies,
> and small this field
> where autumn dies
> yet so richly endowed is no other field under the skies.

It was at Wooler, now quite a few years ago, that I had first
felt the essential kinship between the two peoples on each side of
the Border line. What I had read and heard of Flodden drove it
home. Dacre complained of the flight of the men of Tynemouth
and Bamburghshire, and the Bishop of Durham wrote to Wolsey:

If it were God's pleasure and the King's I would all Horsemen on
the Borders were in France with you, for there should they do much

good; whereas here they do none, but much harm; rifling and rob-
bing as well on our side as of the Scots. . . . and they took divers
prisoners of ours and delivered them to the Scots.

I have good friends in Wooler. They have shown me glens and
streams on their side of the Border, some of which are even lovelier
than those of my own: College Water, where a wild ravine climbs
up to Hen Hole and the Border line, hiding place of " Black
Adam of Cheviot," a notorious reiver; the meeting of the waters
of College and Bowmont at Kirknewton where Bowmont becomes
the Glen, and the hill of Yeavering Bell rises above, crowned with
an ancient settlement where great Saxon kings held court and a
Christian princess gave the new Faith its first foothold on the
Border line; Langleydale, where primitive alder and oak fringe
the tumbling burn and Cheviot lifts its great hulk from the green
and sheltered vale.

One friend had climbed Cheviot forty times, but a reading of
Defoe's description of his arduous climb had been enough for me.
There is no real peak, just a flat boggy plateau.

I had a great desire to see more of Till and to see how Bowmont
behaved as an English stream, and find its junction with Till.
This junction takes place within the private grounds of Ewart
Park, and permission had to be obtained.

Ewart House, like so many of the old Border mansions now
stands empty and the beautiful gardens returned to the wild. But
the woods are still lovely and the wide view to the Cheviots
unspoiled. In the foreground too is Humbleton (Homildon) Hill
where a Percy defeated a Douglas. Within the grounds, close to the
mouth of the Glen, legend says Arthur fought one of his twelve
northern battles.

This was the home of Horace St Paul who in 1798 formed the
Cheviot Legion, a corps of volunteers like their Scottish counter-
part, to help repel the threatened French invasion.

I had not bothered to look at my map. I had been told the
junction of Bowmont with Till was a little over a mile from the
house, " more if you follow its windings closely." I did not see the
water until I stood directly above it on a bank, so deep was it
sunk in a channel of sand. I would never have recognised my
Scottish hill burn in this calm, flat-bottomed stream if I had not
been told. It was always out of sight unless I walked on the edge

K

of the bank, so that the next turn was hidden, so serpentine was its windings. I pushed on fascinated by its unlikeness to any Border stream I had ever followed. There were numerous attractive little sandy beaches, large enough to moor a boat. Its current was almost as slow as Till. . . . Was it Till? I looked at my watch. I had been following that " mile " for over an hour. Only once had I cut a corner. There perhaps I had missed the junction. I threw a twig into the water to test the direction of the current. It flowed north, and very, very slowly.

XII

The Roman Frontier

THE Scottish Border ballads wander back and forth over the Border line: so does much of Border history. It was to follow up some of these threads that I decided to make a deeper and longer sally into Northumberland. It had to be within the short compass of three days, when my niece was on holiday and could take me in her car.

We took the Wooler road but did not stop until near Alnwick. We paused for a picnic lunch and a backward look at the Cheviots. My sister remarked on the prosperous look of the farmland we had come through. Across the wide open spaces, which always impress me on the Northumberland side, the Cheviots looked more than ever a great rampart rising against the skyline. It looked the natural and logical Border line if there had to be one at all, yet it had never really divided the peoples on each side. The Romans had been compelled to set their line farther south, from Tynemouth to Bowness on Solway, to contain, if they could not conquer, those wild tribes of the north. Anglo Bernicia and Deira arose on either side and, united, became the dominant kingdom of the " England " then emerging, challenging the south in power and prestige and withstanding longest the Norman conqueror, though he laid it waste again and again. The Northumbrians, says Howard Pease, " may be said to have been born to rebellion, to have rebellion thrust on them, and finally to have achieved rebellion whenever opportunity offered." But their opposition was to the south; their sympathies lay with their northern neighbours.

Fugitives from Scotland were given refuge in Northumberland, and vice versa. Malcolm, son of the murdered Duncan, was helped to his throne by Siward, Earl of Northumberland, and Cospatrick, a later Earl, fled to Scotland and became Earl of Dunbar.

It was the Northumbrian king, Oswald—in whose reign

Northumbria reached its peak of greatness—who, having fled to Iona, brought the first Christian missionary from that Isle. Aidan founded his monastery on Lindisfarne, off the coast of Northumbria in sight, and under the protection, of the Bernician capital of Bamburgh; and later to Lindisfarne came Cuthbert. Born in the Lammermuir hills he carried his evangelism through the Border hills on both sides.

It was not until Scotland and England each became a kingdom under one king that the division began.

Alnwick looms large in Scottish history. Here one Scottish king, Malcolm Canmore, was killed and another, William the Lion, captured with dire consequences to Scottish independence.

Malcolm—one of Scotland's truly great kings—who had married the Saxon princess Margaret and sheltered her brother, had many times invaded the north of England in support of his wife's relatives against the Normans, ravaging Northumberland and taking so many captives that it was said by the old chroniclers that there was scarcely a Scots household that did not have an English slave.

On his fifth and last expedition he had with him his two sons, Edward, the heir, and his younger brother Edgar. His queen, like the later Margaret, had begged him not to go.

Alnwick Castle was besieged and reduced, but afterwards on the outskirts Malcolm was ambushed and killed. Edward was so grieviously wounded that he died on reaching the forest of Jedburgh, at a spot traditionally known as Edward's Lee, but Malcolm's body was found on the battlefield by two peasants and taken in a farm cart to Tynemouth. So ended the last of the Celtic Scottish kings.

But the Celtic strain was never lost. Both Balliol and Bruce claimed descent from Duncan, and that direct descent from Celtic kings can be traced down to our reigning Queen Elizabeth. It is also worth noting that although Scottish kings have been slain in battle, murdered, or deposed, a foreign king has never usurped the throne.

William the Lion was so called because he was the first Scots king to adopt the Lion Rampant—also the distinctive badge of Northumberland, which county he claimed in right of his grandfather David I, who had married the grand-daughter of the great Siward. David's son, the " peerless prince " Henry, became Earl of Northumberland, and his son, Malcolm " the Maiden " on becoming king relinquished to the King of England his claim to Northumberland.

William the Lion, in his turn King of Scots, could not brook this, and he took the opportunity to invade England in support of the eldest son of Henry II who had rebelled against his father.

William laid siege to Alnwick Castle, but employed a waiting period in tilting with his knights under the castle walls and was surprised by an English relief contingent which had approached the town under cover of a thick fog.

In the fight which followed the King's horse fell and he was pinned beneath. He was manacled, his legs tied beneath his horse's belly, and led from the field.

Put in chains in the castle of Falaise in Normandy, a treaty was extorted from him in which he acknowledged Henry as lord of all Scotland and himself a vassal king. The shame of it cut deep in Scotland. But Richard I of England, another " Lion " king, cared more for money for his Crusade than a Scottish kingdom and sold it back for 10,000 merks, restoring " to his dearest cousin his castles in Scotland as his own by hereditary right ... the Marches of Scotland also to be restored." The two " Lions " became firm friends, the two countries enjoyed a period of peace and amity, and Fordun records that travellers passed freely and unmolested through either country.

Alnwick Castle was not open to the public the day we arrived, so we only saw it from " without the walls." This was the stronghold of the " proud Percies "—though they were not the first owners—the great rivals of the Douglases. They have a long and picturesque history, the very stuff of romance. Hotspur is one of the undying names in medieval history.

One Earl Henry married Eleanor, daughter of John, Earl Warrene. Their son showed the spirit of the Borderer when Edward I sent his commission to the north. " What proof had he of right to his land ? " was the demand.

He drew his old sword.

" This is my title; my ancestors obtained these lands with this good sword, and by this sword I shall keep them! "

How neatly this parallels the " Sang o' the Outlaw Murray " of Ettrick Forest:

" The King of Scotland sent me here,
    And, gude outlaw, I'm sent to thee;
I wad wat of wham ye ªhaud your lands,   ª *hold*
    Or, man, wha may thy master be? "

" ªThir lands are mine," the Outlaw said,   ª *this*
    " I own na king in Christentie;
Frae Soudron I this forest wan,
    When the king nor's knichts were not to
        see. . . .

" Like as I wan them, sae I will keep them
    Contrair all kings in Christentie."

A Percy was in almost all the encounters with Scotland, national or local. But Douglas and Hotspur fought together at Shrewsbury, where Hotspur was killed. There are several ballads connected with the Percies, including the glorious " Chevy Chase," where the Percy is slain. " The Rising of The North," and " Northumberland Betrayed by Douglas " have to do with the Catholic rebellion in support of Mary Queen of Scots. The betrayal of the Earl of Northumberland, who had taken refuge in Liddesdale, by the connivance of Martin Elliot and Hector Armstrong, in which the Armstrong got the blame, led to the expression " To take Hector's cloak " as the strongest term of reprobation.

In the Wars of the Roses the Percies supported the Red Rose. The male line failed with the eleventh earl, and the present dukes are descended from the female side. Not until this century were the age-old rival Border families united by marriage when the Lady Elizabeth Montague Douglas Scott, daughter of the Duke of Buccleuch, became Duchess of Northumberland.

Alnwick is even more medieval-looking than Jedburgh, with its ancient castle and churches, narrow cobbled streets, houses rebuilt with the same old stones, and Hotspur's Tower calling halt to the modern traffic. That day the booths were set up in the old market square, accentuating the medieval atmosphere.

As we climbed out of Alnwick the view became more extensive, the sense of space and freedom increased. The Cheviots were still the great horizon line of hills unchallenged by any intervening peak, such as the Eildons and Ruberslaw on the other side. The craggy cliffs of the Simonside hills were drawing closer. At their feet and on to Carter Bar lay the wilder country, that of the English reivers.

Rothbury, " capital of beautiful Coquetdale," and the wonderful natural park of Cragside, creation of the first Lord Armstrong, proved a pleasant interlude before we were up and out again on the moors—magnificent, horizon-reaching. The few scattered, uncompromising stone houses seemed to scorn even the amenities of gardens and shelter woods, reminding me of Stevenson's " A naked house, a naked moor . . . Yet shall your ragged moor receive the incomparable pomp of eve." Only when we descended to Cambo did we strike softer and greener land—passing Wallington Hall, home of G. M. Trevelyan, an eighteenth-century house and the largest National Trust property in England. The English version of " Fair Mary of Wallington " is localised in Northumberland, but there are several Scottish versions also.

In the fading light of the April day we reached Chollerford, and were so enchanted by our first sight of the North Tyne under its old stone bridge that we decided to stop here and make it our base for exploration. We knew that the best-preserved stretch of the Wall runs between Chollerford and Gilsland by Wade's military road and that we were in fact only half a mile from one of the finest Roman camps, Chesters.

But it was not until we were taking a stroll later and I stopped to lean over the bridge that I realised that this was the Chollerford of the ballad: " Jock o' the Syde."

> At the Choler-ford they a' licht doun,
>   And there, wi' the help o the licht o the moon,
> A tree they cut, wi' fifteen naggs upo' ilk side,
>   To climb up the wa' o' Newcastle toun.

How vivid it all seemed here! They had ridden all that way from Liddesdale down through the North Tynedale pass and from here to Newcastle to rescue their " billy."

Next morning we recrossed the bridge and headed back for Heddon-on-the-Wall, along Wade's Road, into which he put the stones of the then existing section of the Wall—according to his lights, put them to better use. The broad vallum still stretches beside the road.

My own interest in the Wall had been aroused, not by textbooks at school, but by Kipling's *Puck of Pook's Hill*, and I was glad in later years to find that Trevelyan gives Kipling full marks as a historian.

Heddon-on-the-Wall, built on the site of a Roman mile-castle, had not much to show, but from there we followed increasingly attractive country, the straight road rising and falling in a series of swells as a Northumbrian road so often does.

At Corbridge we touched the Tyne again, but broader now with the united waters of the North and South Tynes, and still as fresh as a mountain stream.

The stone bridge here, of seven arches, was the only one to withstand the floods of 1771. Perhaps the balladist did not exaggerate when he said that at Chollerford " the waters ran like mountains hie." At Corbridge there had been a wooden bridge built in 1235, and it is still possible, we are told, to see the oaken tie beams at low water. Traces of the ten stone piers of the Agricolan Bridge, which carried Dere Street on its way to the Borders, can also be seen under favourable conditions.

The Anglo-Saxons who followed seem to have founded a settlement here, and were reputed to have left much treasure. It was for this treasure and Roman gold coins that King John " searched " the town in 1201.

A board at the entrance to the bridge gives an excellent summary of the town's eventful history—a procedure which I would recommend to other historical towns.

Corbridge was, of course, the great Roman camp of Corstopitum. It was there before the Wall was built. Agricola built it as a cavalry fort about A.D. 79, as a base for his advance north, but it grew into a large military and civil town. He pressed north, forming his chain of forts, as far as Perthshire. Somewhere there was fought the battle of Mons Graupius, the first historical instance where the native peoples lost the battle by coming down from their heights. But that proved the northern limit of what Leonard Cottrell calls " the penetration, though not the conquest, of Scotland." Continual trouble followed with attacks from the north and this led to the building of the Wall, on the advice of Hadrian when he arrived on a tour of inspection in 121–2. It took only seven years to complete and was $73\frac{1}{2}$ miles long, and like everything the Romans did was logical and straightforward—so unlike the Border line, also from sea to sea. The Wall was shaped in unity of purpose, the Border line in disunity.

Hexham, our next stopping-place, has that medieval look, too, which seems to be better preserved in England. The Abbey dominates one side of the square and the Moot Hall the other, and the stone houses look as old as in Alnwick. The Saxons robbed the Roman Wall to build their church and when it fell temporarily into decay the people robbed the church to build their houses.

Built in 1115, the Priory was several times severely damaged and despoiled by the Scottish armies, the worst being by David II in 1346. It will be recalled that the flag captured at Hornshole by the Hawick callants was emblazoned with a gold cross on a blue background and bore the arms of the Priory of St Andrew of Hexham. In 1908 the captured flag came home. When the reconstructed nave of the Abbey was opened, Hawick was represented in the procession by its Provost. He carried a replica of the flag and afterwards presented it to the Hexham Abbey authorities.

Within the Abbey we saw links with the Romans: a memorial to a young soldier of only twenty-five who had yet seen seven years service, which Bishop Wilfrid brought from Corstopitum, and a Saxon font hollowed out of a Roman pillar.

Wilfrid appears on a panel as the first bishop, Cuthbert follows. Wilfrid had a lot to do with Border history—he was born at Ripon, in the Deira of Northumbria, as Cuthbert was born in Bernicia, about 634. Educated first at Lindisfarne, he later came under the influence of the Roman church. Now the Lindisfarne church was Celtic while the Roman church was national. Aidan had brought the Christianity of Columba from Iona to another " holy isle ": " to the hills these northern saints lifted up their eyes, and to their ears the litany of the ocean was antiphonal."

The uses of their religion, however, differed from that of the Roman, in small matters as in large. King Oswy, who had succeeded Oswald and who had united Bernicia and Deira into one province, was largely swayed by his wife who observed the Roman usage. He called the Synod of Whitby to decide the difference after Wilfrid had ejected from Ripon all those monks who would not conform, including Cuthbert.

This is one of the weighty scenes in British history. The small Celtic church faced the great universal church of Rome. Said Wilfrid: " Though your fathers were holy, do you think that a small band of men in a corner of a remote island is to be preferred to the Universal Church of Christ? " The decision was given in

favour of the Church of St Peter " who held the keys of the kingdom " as against the church founded by Columba. Cuthbert in
the cause of peace and unity conformed to the decision. But towards the end of his life he abandoned his bishopric and retired to
his cell on the Farne Islands off the coast of Bamburgh.

Colman of Lindisfarne, with all his Scottish followers and some
Englishmen, departed for Iona. It was the first " walk-out " of
the Scottish Church. But Oswy, remembering what Northumbria
owed to the church of Columba, appointed an Irish Celtic priest,
but he died within the year. He was the last Celtic bishop over
the Northumbrian church.

Trevelyan has said of these first Lindisfarne Celtic priests:
" the ascetic, yet cheerful life of these ardent, lovable, unworldly
apostles of the moorland who tramped the heather all day to
preach by the burnside at evenings won the hearts of the men of
the north."

It is salutary for a Scot to explore Northumberland and hear the
other side of the story of fire and foray. Hexham seemed to attract
more trouble than most. Wallace during a period of famine in
the north marched into Cumberland and Northumberland, col-
lecting much plunder and, according to English chroniclers,
committing many cruelties. In all this Hexham was caught up,
and also in the Wars of the Roses.

On the Hexham Levels above the town was fought the battle of
Hexham where the Lancastrians were defeated by the Yorkists,
and Queen Margaret, wife of Henry VI, fled with her infant son to
the woods. There she was succoured by a Scottish reiver, and
helped in her flight into Scotland.

Now we were following the South Tyne, through exceedingly
pleasant country to Haydon Bridge, Bardon Mill and Haltwhistle.
We were into the region of the Ridleys, who, like the Percies, were
often over the Border as well as at war with neighbours. But the
Ridleys of Unthank Hall gave Nicholas Ridley, Bishop of London,
who was burned at the stake in 1555, and the Ridleys and Feather-
stones lost their lands in the Royalist cause.

The main road, we found, bypassed Old Haltwhistle itself, so
we missed the thirteenth-century church, which must be unique in
that it passed practically unscathed through all the raids. It was
from this district the Armstrongs carried off Carey's cow.

We were not far from Carlisle now, and Harribee, the hanging hill. The English Borderers of this region were almost as obnoxious to one Bishop of Carlisle. Writing to Cardinal Wolsey in 1522 he said: " There is more theft, more extortion by English thieves than there is by all the Scots of Scotland." At the other end of the Wall, at Newcastle, for a long time it was forbidden to accept apprentices from Redesdale and Tynedale, so evil was the reputation of that region.

The gates of Newcastle were closed again against the men of Tynedale and Redesdale in the rebellion of 1715. One Thomas Armstrong (" Luck-in-the-bag "), and a Captain Hunter were together in Lord Derwentwater's army, whose standard had been raised, and King James proclaimed on the North Fells on 6 October. Perhaps that Armstrong atoned for the betrayal of the Earl of Northumberland.

At Brampton the English linked up with the Scottish. The Scots wanted to fight on their own soil, the Highlanders resisted every step that took them further over the Border even with the promise of a 6*d.* a day wage! But General Foster's will prevailed and the armies went forward to Preston—and defeat.

Derwent, Collingwood, Hall of Otterburn, were among those executed. Two of the Swinburnes of Capheaton, ancestors of the poet, were imprisoned and one died. General Foster and Nithsdale escaped from prison through the wit of their womenfolk. Foster's sister took the local blacksmith to London to forge a false key: Nithsdale's wife got him out disguised in her own clothes; Macintosh escaped through his own prowess, he and some friends knocking out the turnkey of Newgate. This exploit was celebrated in a ballad, and another ballad tells the story of the gallant and popular Lord Derwentwater, whose execution made a deep impression on the Borders. Young Charles Radcliffe, who was in the second Jacobite rising, is also celebrated in a ballad. Brampton was again the scene of a gathering of the 1745 rebels.

But before we actually came to Brampton we turned up by Greenhead to Gilsland, crossing the Pennine Way. We were again in the old kingdom of Strathclyde, now Cumberland.

Scott was here in 1797, carrying his " raids " south of the Border line and finding material for *The Bridal of Triermain*. Here, too, he took a young lady to see the Wall, found some flowers growing there and presented them to her with some very juvenile verses. But that young lady was not Charlotte, and we hear no more of her.

Charlotte was to appear later at Gilsland, in a manner best calculated to win his instant admiration—a spirited rider on a spirited horse.

From Gilsland it was only a short climb of about a mile or so to the fort of Camboglanna (Birdoswald), lying on the line of the Wall. The Roman remains are slight here, but the view is magnificent; over the valley of the Tyne to the Pennine hills; to the east the Whin Sill and to the north the wild country leading to the Bewcastle Fells and the Debatable Land. How wild and desolate that northern land must have seemed to the Romans, and it had never really been tamed for centuries after they had gone.

This quiet side road led down to Lanercost and the Priory whose chronicle has recorded so much of Border history. It lies in a green little vale, and here the road branched, the left turn going by Naworth, Dacres stronghold, but both leading to Brampton. This was to be our terminal, so we returned to Greenhead to join the military road running straight to Chollerford. This road is parallel with the best-preserved part of the Wall, which can be reached easily. Most of it is within the Northumberland National Park.

A feeling of loneliness still hangs over this rather bleak moorland road, with the fells rising and falling on either side and only a few scattered farmhouses and one inn, the " Twice Brewed," which looked old enough to have once known highwaymen and smugglers. But there is a Youth Hostel, and further along the road a guest house. From there it was but a step up to the Wall. The Northumberland County Council have provided a car park just beside it. Already—as early as April—there were quite a number of cars, and several groups of people were strolling up and down on the top of the Wall, which is low and well preserved and topped with turf. It was all too easy. I had imagined the Wall running over wild uplands, windy and empty, taking some effort to reach.

Feeling slightly deflated we returned to the main road, undecided whether to visit Housesteads further on—said to be the best preserved of all the forts on the Wall, and having a museum and guide.

But as we cruised on we saw no signpost: then we saw two parked cars and a gate into a field. On a sudden impulse we got out to investigate. A track led from the gate beside a burn that seemed to come down through a gap in the Whin Sill, and lead to a lonely farmhouse. Beyond the farmhouse there was a wood climbing the hill and we made a rough guess that the Wall must be somewhere there, if not Housesteads itself.

When we skirted the end of the wood there it was—the great wall climbing up and up out of sight. It was higher here, higher than our heads and it was a scramble to get on top. The dressed stones of the face were set in good order but here and there the turf-topped surface had crumbled and walking along the top became more precarious. We followed it as it rose and fell, but always continuing to ascend. We were absolutely alone up there—the wall stretched on behind and beyond as if it had no beginning and no end. We were but infinitesimal specks in a vast space clinging to a tightrope slung across the top of the world. . . .

And that is why, because this was for us the Wall, we did not stop again when further along the military way we saw the Ministry of Works signboard and groups of people following the path up to Housesteads. And that is how a Roman " must " came to be left out of our programme.

Next day we had to return home and we decided to go by way of Kielder Forest into Liddesdale.

It was a reluctant farewell to Northumberland. Over the years —for I had spent many happy days at Bamburgh and Wooler— and in my late shorter forays after the ballads, I had grown to love that land which in so many ways seemed like my own. Indeed I have never felt a stranger in Northumberland.

But I had found no Common Ridings or Border Festivals as on the Scottish side. Had Howard Pease, himself a Northumbrian, partly given the answer?

> The Northumbrians are not careful like the Scots of their patrimony of romance. Sir Walter treasured up all the tales and traditions of the countryside. . . . They [the Northumbrians] are essentially a practical race—lovers of adventure yet wedded to facts, not dreams. . . . The Rev. George Hodgkin, their chief historian, would not have the Waverley novels in his house.

But he then goes on to compare the many other characteristics common to both races, " born of Border strife and harsh environment, which still endure and were often in evidence in the Great War."

Still there was Swinburne, the poet—" a mosstrooper out of Sappho," Howard Pease had called him.

The time had been too short to have all the answers. But " there is always tomorrow."

It was one of these pearl-like April mornings when we left Chollerford, the mists rising from the river and the dew still heavy on the grass.

We stopped to have a look at Chesters. The custodian said the museum was closed indefinitely, but we did not greatly care. The morning was too lovely to spend within walls. Everything was beginning to sparkle in the intensifying sunlight. The beautifully chiselled walls of the bath house gleamed. Sheep grazed placidly on the rich meadow grass between the excavations.

Margery, who is the archaeologist of the family, went off to examine the excavations and take photographs. Kate became intrigued by some Erinus Alpinus she discovered growing in the walls, plants which are certainly not indigenous to this country. I wandered down to the river bank to have a last look at Tyne. It was shallow and clear over its stones, and fringed with trees that drooped their April green to the water's edge. The air was lambent. It was all so incomparably lovely, peaceful and still.

> Sleepe after toyle, port after stormy seas,
> Ease after warre . . . does greatly please.

APPENDIX

Tunes of some of the Ballads
Quoted in this Book

Johnie Armstrong[1]

[1] These two tunes are both taken from F. J. Child, *The English and Scottish Popular Ballads*, v. 420.

Dick o' the Cow[2]

[2] This tune is taken from Alexander Campbell, *Albyn's Anthology*, II. 30.

Jock o' the Side[3]

[3] This tune is taken from Alexander Campbell, *Albyn's Anthology*, II. 28.

Goodnight and joy be wi' ye all[4]

[4] This tune is taken from Robert Chambers, *The Songs of Scotland prior to Burns*, p. 273.

Kinmont Willie[5]

[5] This tune is taken from Alexander Campbell, *Albyn's Anthololgy*. I. 78.

Index